Doughnuts, Letters,  Midnight Phone Calls

Doughnuts, Letters, & Midnight Phone Calls

Making Connections with Youth

ANNETTE PAXMAN BOWEN

Deseret Book Company
Salt Lake City, Utah

Library of Congress Cataloging-in-Publication Data

Bowen, Annette Paxman, 1952–
    Doughnuts, letters, and midnight phone calls : making connections
with youth / Annette Paxman Bowen.
        p.   cm.
    ISBN 0-87579-561-7
    1. Church work with youth — Mormon Church.   I. Title.
BX8643.Y6B68   1991
259′.23 — dc20   91-32828
                                                                         CIP

Printed in the United States of America
10   9   8   7   6   5   4   3   2

For My Kids—
You know who you are—
and
Margaret M. Muth,
who taught me to write

Contents

Contents

Prologue

Cast thy bread upon the waters: for thou shalt find it after many days.

— *Ecclesiastes 11:1*

I was doing the morning's dishes when the phone rang. I wiped my hands. "Hello?"

"Oh, good! You're home. You've got to hear this."

It was Brenda, calling long-distance.

"You won't believe what Kendrick did this morning. I left him in the middle of the living room floor and went back to my bedroom. He can barely roll over, so I figured he'd be okay. Anyway, I could hear him making happy noises, so I knew he was all right."

I smiled, remembering the happy baby sounds of my own children.

"So, when I walk back in the living room, there's Kendrick. He's managed somehow to move clear across the room. I don't know how he got there—he must have rolled. Anyway, he's lodged up against the bookcase, and he's *covered* with straw!"

I laughed, picturing this sight.

Brenda continued, "I have a basket full of curly straw with some of my tole-painted wooden eggs in it sitting on the bottom shelf. I haven't put away all the stuff from the low shelves yet, because I didn't think he could get to it. Well, Kendrick had seen those eggs and gone after them. Then he'd pulled and stretched the straw until he'd covered himself with it. You should've seen him! He had it in his hair, his clothes, between his toes—even down in his diaper. Everywhere! He looked like a scarecrow."

"I hope you took some pictures."

"I did. I wish I could've left him looking like that for Tim to see, but he won't be home for hours. He'll have to settle for the pictures. But, that's not the only reason why I'm calling. Hang on a second, okay?"

"Sure," I agreed. I heard Brenda fumbling with something.

"Oh, I hope this works. Okay, are you ready?"

"Yes." I waited for whatever surprise she had for me that prompted this expensive, middle-of-the-day phone call. I heard something whir and then in a few moments, I heard a tiny infant voice repeating a simple syllable.

"Da, da. Da, da, da." I was genuinely surprised how moved I was by that tiny voice: I felt tears welling in my eyes.

"Those are his first words!" Brenda shrieked. "He just said them while I was cleaning him up! Tim's going to hate himself for missing the real event, but at least I caught it on tape. Of course, he'll *love* it that Kendrick said his name first!"

"How did you manage to record it?"

"Luckily, the changing table is near the desk, and the tape recorder was sitting right there. I don't even know what else is on this tape. I just grabbed the recorder and waited for Kendrick to say something. It took about two minutes, but then he started up again. Isn't it fantastic?"

"It's wonderful!" I assured Brenda.

"Well, I've gotta go. This call will cost me a fortune."

"Hey, thanks for sharing this with me," I tell her. "You can reverse the charges next time." She had done that in the past, with my coaxing. Before she said good-bye and hung up, I told her, as I always do, that I love her.

As I turned back to my dishes, I thought about Brenda and Tim and, now, this infant, Kendrick, and how much they add to my life. I am not Brenda's mother, mother-in-law, sister, or aunt. We are close friends. Our friendship began ten years ago when I was Brenda's and Tim's early-morning seminary teacher.

I ran through the names and faces of other dear friends of mine: the faces of students I've taught over the years. And I counted the years: I've worked with teenagers for eighteen years, with only two short stints in Relief Society callings wedged in.

They have been years filled with more lessons, meetings, activity nights, sleep overs, ball games, youth conferences, dances, roadshows, camps, and planning sessions than I can count. I've laughed till my stomach hurt and cried till my makeup washed away; I've leapt out of bed with excitement and anticipation, and I've collapsed onto my couch, completely exhausted; I've cooked pizza, spaghetti, hot dogs, and pancakes and mixed more high-sugar punch than anyone should have to confess; I've said, "I'm burned out. I can't do this anymore," yet one hour later, after being with My Kids, I've said, "Please don't ever release me from this calling."

Most important, I've spent countless hours doing the most important thing a friend of teenagers can do: I've listened. And, through the listening, I have learned much. Because of the grand paradox of teaching, I have headed many times into classrooms armed with stories, scriptures, principles, and love, and ended up learning the most.

Many lessons I've learned as an adult have been taught to me by my young friends. "Cast thy bread upon the waters: for thou shalt find it after many days" (Ecclesiastes 11:1). I've cast many handfuls of bread upon the water. Years later, much of that bread has been found and multiplied. Rich, plentiful, and satisfying, this bread has come back to me as greater understanding of many eternal truths. It has come as experiences that have brought deep, abiding joy. It has come as pleasures and privileges, such as hearing baby Kendrick's first coherent words.

Within the covers of this book are many rewarding and sometimes painful experiences I've had with individual teenagers as I've worked beside them. The stories that compose this book illustrate gospel principles that, together, my young friends and I have found to be true. These are true stories of real people. To protect their privacy, however, I have changed the names.

These stories are told to you as I experienced them. They are stories I know are true because I was there. Please look to the experiences and lessons themselves and watch for the hand of the Lord in these young people's lives, the miraculous work of the Holy Spirit and the truths made evident through living the gospel.

Answering Calls

And now, verily, verily, I say unto thee, put your trust in that Spirit which leadeth to do good—yea, to do justly, to walk humbly, to judge righteously; and this is my Spirit...

— *Doctrine & Covenants 11:12*

Robert.

I hear his name and instantly I remember that night, the call, and his voice, although it's been more than a decade since I stood in my kitchen at two in the morning to answer the phone.

I remember tiny details: the humid night air, the frog croaking from a corner of my patio, the lights in the pool across the park illuminating the turquoise water.

It was Saturday. We'd entertained guests who had stayed past midnight. Scott and I had cleared the table and washed the dishes, and then he'd gone to bed around one. Because our ward had late Sunday meetings, I knew I could sleep in the next morning, so I stayed up another hour to enjoy the silence of the house—a rare hour of peace for me, a mother of active preschoolers.

I wasn't alarmed when the phone rang, because Scott was a medical resident who often covered the emergency room. Our phone frequently rang in the night. I was surprised, however, when I heard Robert's voice.

"Sister Bowen?"

Robert was one of my Sunday School students. I'd also taught him in early-morning seminary for a couple of years, so I knew his voice well.

"Sorry to call so late. Did I wake you up?" he continued.

"No. You know what a night-owl I am, if I can get away with it. Did you drive by and see my lights on?"

"No," Robert said.

There was something different about his voice, so I asked, "Robert, are you okay?"

"I'm fine." His voice was suddenly robust. "I'm fine," he repeated. Robert was a superb actor who often played lead roles in high school productions, so I knew he was capable of covering up something wrong.

"Are you sure?"

"Really, I'm all right," he assured me. "The reason I'm calling is that I know you can see the clubhouse from your front windows. Sorry to bother you, but we had a cast party there tonight, and I'm wondering if anyone is still there. Can you see if any lights are on?"

"Sure, no problem." I walked into my living room and looked across the park at the darkened windows of the community clubhouse. As I returned to the kitchen, it struck me as odd that Robert would call to ask such a question—at this hour, wouldn't a kid normally drive by to check to see if a party was still going on, rather than risk waking up an entire household? Besides, there was a midnight curfew for clubhouse activities, and I was pretty sure Robert knew that, too.

I picked up the phone again. "The clubhouse is dark, Robert. The party would've had to end at midnight, anyway. You know the rules."

"Oh, that's right. I forgot. So, nobody's there?"

"Nobody's there. Only the night lights around the pool are on." I asked again, "Are you sure you're okay? I know your folks are gone. Do you have anybody staying with you?"

Robert hesitated. "Uh, no. No, I don't have anybody with me."

Again, there was something strange about his voice.

"Well, okay, then." My mind raced to figure out what had really prompted this call. "But if you want to come over, you can. In fact, if you'd rather stay here till your parents get home, you're more than welcome."

"Thanks, but I'm okay. Listen, I'll let you go so that you can get to bed. I didn't realize how late it was."

"Are you *sure* you're all right?" I asked again. I did not feel that Robert was squaring with me.

"I'm fine. I'll talk to you tomorrow. 'Bye." Suddenly, he couldn't get off the phone fast enough.

I was perplexed. That story about the clubhouse was pretty lame. I walked into the living room again and looked at the clubhouse. I was a member of the homeowners board of directors, and the security guard had told me that teenagers occasionally hid in the sauna or behind a pool wall to avoid detection so that they could swim after the pool closed.

I opened my front door to listen for splashing or the Jacuzzi motor, sounds that usually carried across the park in the still of the night. Nothing. No one was over there.

Then I received the prompting: call Robert back. Better still, drive to his house and check on him. I glanced at my watch. Two fifteen. I went into the kitchen, picked up the phone, and hesitated. I'd asked Robert several times if he was okay, and he had said he was. He was in high school: old enough to take care of himself. I hung up the phone, flipped off the kitchen light, and went upstairs to check on my children.

7

As I pulled the covers up over my oldest son, the thought came again: call Robert back. If he were my son, and I was out of town, I'd appreciate someone checking on him.

I went down to the kitchen, turned on the light, and picked up the phone. I dialed Robert's number; but before it rang, I put the receiver back on the hook. Robert would think I was crazy. What senior in high school wanted his Sunday School teacher bugging him at this hour? He'd probably hung up after calling me and gone straight to bed. He was probably sound asleep by now. Whatever he had wanted would certainly wait till morning. I'd make a point of pulling him aside at church tomorrow.

As I walked down the hall to my bedroom, I thought, once again, that it really wouldn't hurt for me to drive past Robert's house to see if there were any lights on. If I thought he was still up, maybe I'd go knock on the door—maybe, then, he'd talk. If the house was dark, he wouldn't even have to know I'd checked on him.

I opened the bedroom closet to grab the shoes I'd kicked off before doing the dishes.

"What are you doing?" my husband mumbled sleepily.

"I'm getting some shoes," I whispered.

"What on earth for?" he asked.

"I'm just going to go drive past Robert's house to make sure he's okay. His parents are out of town, and I got a weird phone call from him a little while ago."

Scott flipped on his reading lamp. "What?" He sat up, squinting in the light.

I told Scott about the phone call and the feeling I'd had. "Am I crazy?" I asked.

He nodded. "You're nuts! Forget it. The kid is asleep in bed by now. I'll bet he didn't realize how late it was, and all he really wanted was to know if the party was still going. You can talk to him in the morning, if you're still worried."

I felt like an idiot.

Before I climbed into bed, I said a quick prayer, asking for Robert's safety and protection.

Scott nudged me awake late the next morning.

"Sorry to get you up, sleepyhead, but the bishop wants to talk to you."

"Why?"

"Beats me. Here's the phone."

"Hello, Annette? Brother Perez just called to say he's sending Robert to talk to me. Said he got a weird phone call from Robert last night, and then Robert knocked on his door first thing this morning. Robert told him he'd called you last night, too. Any clue what this is about? You know how I hate surprises."

I told him about the phone call and my "funny" feelings.

"So, did you drive over there?" he asked.

"No. I almost did, but it was so late and it seemed a pretty crazy thing to do, so I just went to bed. I thought I'd talk to Robert today and suggest that he stay with us until his parents get home."

"Hmm," the bishop thought for a minute. "That's not a bad idea. Well, talk to you later."

I was worried, but there wasn't anything I could do about it. If something was wrong with Robert, the bishop would handle it.

At church, I watched for Robert. He wasn't at the sacrament table, his usual post. In fact, I couldn't see him anywhere in the chapel. Just as the meeting started, I saw him slip into the back row of the chapel. It was obvious that he'd been crying.

Something had happened last night. Those "funny feelings" I'd experienced must have been promptings. I groaned inwardly.

Sacrament meeting lasted forever. I wanted to talk to Brother Perez. What had Robert said to him?

After sacrament meeting, I didn't have to look for Brother Perez: he found me. "I understand you got a call from Robert early this morning."

I nodded. "You got one too?"

"Yeah. You know what that does to you when the phone rings in the middle of the night. I prepared myself for the worst, and then I heard Robert's voice."

"What did he say?"

"He said that he just called to talk, but he could tell he woke me up, so he said he'd let me go back to sleep. Then he hung up."

"What time was it?" I asked.

"I checked the clock. It was around two, I think."

I told Brother Perez about my phone call and the feelings I'd had.

"You know what?" he responded, "I had those exact same thoughts, but I told myself I was crazy, so I just rolled over and tried to go back to sleep. The thoughts kept coming back—I should call Robert or get up and drive over there, but I was too tired to get up, I told myself, so I'd talk to him in the morning, and I went back to sleep. You can imagine how I felt when he showed up at my house this morning in tears."

"So, what's the deal?" I asked.

Brother Perez stared at his feet. "I really can't tell you." He shook his head slightly. "Robert will probably come and talk to you, but I can't be the one to tell you."

I felt awful, almost nauseated and feverish, like you feel when you're coming down with the flu.

"Would it have made any difference if we'd called him or gone over there last night?" I asked. I really didn't want to hear the answer.

"Yeah." Brother Perez nodded. "It would have made a big difference."

Brother Perez was right. Each of us had been strongly prompted by the Holy Ghost to intercede in someone's life at a crucial time. We had felt prompted, but we'd rationalized away our feelings and failed to act.

The results were devastating.

Robert did talk to me. In a voice I could barely hear, he told me that he had invited a young woman home after the cast party that Saturday night to watch a video with him. She'd told him that she didn't have a curfew and that she could stay all night, if he wanted her to. He hadn't thought that was a very good idea, so after a while, he had excused himself and gone to another room to phone me and Brother Perez. What he had wanted was advice about how to graciously get this girl out of his house before his hormones overruled his brain; however, he'd felt awkward once he had us on the phone, so he'd made up excuses and hung up.

The young woman spent the night.

The next morning, a tearful Robert went to his bishop to confess that he'd broken the law of chastity.

That Sunday morning, Robert began the long and painful process of repentance. The consequences have reached into the years, for Robert learned, long after the fact, that he'd fathered a child, and, without his knowledge, the child had been aborted. He has been tortured by this information.

Knowledge of that fact seared itself across my own soul. I know that Robert is responsible for the choices he made that night, but I also know that I felt prompted to contact Robert after his phone call to me.

Robert. When I think of him, I always remember that night and that phone call. Since then, whenever I get "funny feelings," no matter how unusual or inconvenient the ideas that flash across my mind, I act on them. The Holy Ghost has never been wrong.

"The Spirit itself maketh intercession for us with groanings which cannot be uttered. And he that searcheth the hearts knoweth what is the mind of the Spirit, because he maketh intercession for the saints according to the will of God" (Romans 8:26–27).

When Thou Art Converted

And when thou art converted, strengthen thy brethren.
— Luke 22:32

Sharon Williams was a Mia Maid adviser who magnified her calling. I'd never met anyone who taught with such focus, organization, energy, and enthusiasm. She was a wonder to watch, and I watched her constantly.

We became friends when we worked on a roadshow together. Although I was new to the ward, the bishop asked me to write and direct the show. Sharon was a member of a dynamic Young Women board and helped me tremendously.

As anyone knows who has "done a roadshow," there were many challenges and difficult moments during the months we worked on the show; however, there were blessings, too. One of those blessings was the opportunity to work with Sharon and to watch her in action.

Sharon had the names of fifteen Mia Maids on her roll, but many of them were not attending church. Some teachers might have focused on just the ones who were active, but not Sharon. She met and got to know every Mia Maid on the list. She was tireless.

She trained her class presidency, and together they set the

goal to activate every class member on the roll. They gathered information about each young woman: family background, personal talents and interests, and the kids they hung around with at school. Then they made plans. Sharon wrote notes to each one, telling them about herself and her family and what was happening at church. Members of the class presidency, encouraged by Sharon, approached the class members at school, introducing themselves. They called each girl, each week, to extend invitations. There was never any pressure exerted—just encouraging words and an obvious warm welcome awaiting them.

Slowly, the less active Mia Maids began to respond to the enthusiastic interest being shown them. One wanted to meet the "crazy woman" who was writing notes to her. Another decided to come to activity night to "check it out." Another started eating lunch with some of the more active girls, and finally, one Sunday, she agreed to go with them to church. Sharon was ecstatic.

Marie was one of these young women. Marie finally allowed Sharon to take her to an activity, because she'd run out of excuses.

She liked what she saw. After that first trip to Young Women, Sharon always made sure Marie had a ride to the Mia Maid activities, and before long, Marie consented to being picked up for church on Sundays. Sharon took great pains to make sure Marie was welcomed by everyone she met.

The roadshow coincided with Marie's fledgling weeks at church. Sharon approached me during a roadshow rehearsal.

"I'm wondering if you can use a drummer for the roadshow."

"What?" I asked.

"A drummer. Do you need a drummer for the roadshow music?"

"Sharon, we're not working with live music."

"Well, I need you to think about it, because we need to use

14

Marie as a drummer for the show. She really wants to do it. I've already talked with her about it."

We were having enough problems just getting through rehearsals with tapes of piano music. I hadn't even thought of working with a live band. Sharon was one step ahead of me.

"I'll play the piano for you, if you'll just add Marie as a drummer," Sharon offered. Noting my hesitancy, she added, "Live music will be much better than tapes!"

She was right. That week I gathered sheet music for our songs, and Sharon started practicing. She got the music to Marie, and, before I could catch my breath, we had live music for the roadshow—at least, piano and drums. Sharon, of course, hauled Marie's drums to and from rehearsals in the back of her green station wagon.

"Tell me more about Marie," I asked Sharon one afternoon while we worked on costumes. I was interested in this young woman, who'd told me she wanted to be a professional drummer in a rock band.

Sharon told me all she could about Marie's family: She had one younger brother, Joel, who hadn't been to church. Yet. Her father, a master chief petty officer in the navy, was not a member of the Church. Marie's mother was a member but had not been to church for many years. Someone, at some time, had seen to it that Marie and Joel had been baptized.

"By the way, you should use Marie's mother in the roadshow," Sharon told me.

"How?" I asked.

"I've heard that she's a professional make-up artist, and she's a head sales representative for a big cosmetics company. Don't you think you could use her?"

Of course I could use her, but would she do it? I didn't feel comfortable approaching a total stranger—and a long-time inactive member—to ask her to do a huge job for the roadshow. I was having enough trouble getting active members of the ward to lend a hand.

Sharon, however, was fearless. "I'll bet we could get her to do it. I'll have Marie ask her." Being a big thinker, Sharon didn't stop there. "Maybe we could even get her to donate the makeup for free. Cosmetics companies give away all kinds of free samples."

Sharon was right once again. For our roadshow performances, we not only had live music furnished by Sharon on the piano and Marie on the drums but also had free makeup, donated by a national cosmetics company, and the help of a professional make-up artist, Marie's mother, Nina.

I'd like to say that the family was, from that moment on, active in the Church, but it didn't happen that way.

Marie kept coming to church. She listened carefully to Sharon's lessons and began applying the principles in her life. She started to write a journal. She held interviews with Sharon, where Sharon introduced her to the Young Women's personal progress program. Marie set some short-term and long-term goals for herself.

One goal was to get her brother to come to church with her. At first, Joel wasn't interested. In fact, it took Marie months of effort before Joel finally gave in and agreed to come to church with Marie. Sharon picked them up and took them with her.

Joel was surprised to see several kids he knew from school in his Sunday School class, and he enjoyed meeting with this group. Soon, he was receiving individual instruction from the bishop and his deacons quorum advisor. A few months later, Joel, with the consent of his parents, received the Aaronic Priesthood and was ordained a deacon.

On that Sunday, Marie stood before the congregation to bear

her testimony of the gospel and express her gratitude to Sharon for her love, interest, and support. She spoke of the power of setting goals, and told the story of how she had set the goal and then hoped and prayed and worked for the time Joel would come to church with her. Once that goal was realized, she envisioned the time when Joel would receive the priesthood. She was thrilled that that goal, too, had been attained.

Marie embodied the reality of the admonition of Luke 22:32. She had become converted, and she had, literally, strengthened her brother.

Sharon moved away from our ward the following year. By that time, however, we had forged a friendship that has endured the years and the distance that separated us.

As for Marie and Joel, their testimonies were strong enough to keep them attending church and growing in their understanding of the gospel, even though Sharon wasn't there any more. And, with Sharon gone, Nina began driving her children to church. For months, she simply dropped them off in the parking lot, but one Sunday, she ventured into the building and sat through sacrament meeting with them. It was a good beginning.

Two years later, I had the blessing of being called to teach early-morning seminary. Marie was a Laurel by this time, a senior in high school, and she was in my seminary class.

At age seventeen, Marie was a strong, motivated, and determined young woman. Yes, she was still playing the drums and was a very proficient drummer. She was well-liked and respected at school: she had many friends. She set a good example for everyone who knew her. I particularly appreciated her quiet strength and her great faith. She and Joel had successfully coaxed their mother into attending church with them more often than not.

After Marie's father returned from a long absence on a navy

assignment, Marie told me that she wanted her father to take the missionary discussions. She confided that she had set a couple of goals for herself and her family: she wanted to see her father baptized and then she wanted her family to be sealed in the temple.

I thought it was a tall order, but I did not doubt her ability to do all she could to ensure that these events took place. I had seen Marie accomplish most things she set her mind to do.

Marie's father, Ryan, was impressed by his children's growth and strength, and he agreed to have the missionaries come to his home for lessons. Again. As it turned out, Ryan had received the missionary lessons before. His biggest obstacle was the Word of Wisdom: he had been a smoker and drinker for years.

Marie told me about the night the missionaries challenged her father to obey the Word of Wisdom. Ryan accepted their challenge instantly. He got a large box from storage, gathered all the liquor and cigarettes in the house, and put them in the box. Then he asked the missionaries to dispose of it all for him.

Ryan was a strong-willed man, and though he struggled for a while to overcome his physical habits, he succeeded. About a month later, he accepted another challenge: he would be baptized.

His baptism was a momentous occasion for Marie and for everyone who had grown to love this family. Once again, Marie had realized a goal. With divine assistance and through her faith and example, she had worked patiently to help reactivate her brother, encouraged her mother to to attend church, and now, her father had been baptized. Together, the family set the goal to prepare to go to the temple.

One year later, Marie's dream of dreams came true. Dressed in white, she knelt at an altar in the Los Angeles Temple with her brother, Joel, and her parents, Nina and Ryan. An officiator sealed them, making them "a forever family." Marie had written those words in her journal as a long-term goal when she was a

Mia Maid, just after Sharon had drawn her lovingly into the circle of the Church.

It's been ten years since I attended the sealing of that family. In that time, Joel has finished high school, attended Brigham Young University, and successfully served a mission. Not long ago he married a beautiful, worthy young woman in the Los Angeles Temple.

During this same time, Marie met a wonderful returned missionary at a Church activity, fell in love with him, and married him in the Los Angeles Temple. They are now the devoted parents of three terrific children. Marie still plays the drums. And she runs marathons, realizing another goal she set for herself. The last I heard, she was serving as an adviser in the Young Women program, a position that completes the wonderful cycle of influence that began with Sharon's reaching out to activate every Mia Maid on her class roll.

How long will this cycle of fellowship and leadership continue? No doubt it will spin into the eternities.

Burdens

Wherefore, redemption cometh in and through the Holy Messiah; for he is full of grace and truth. Behold, he offereth himself a sacrifice for sin, to answer the ends of the law, unto all those who have a broken heart and a contrite spirit; and unto none else can the ends of the law be answered.

— 2 Nephi 2:6–7

The seminary manual suggested that for the lesson on the Atonement I take to class a backpack filled with heavy rocks and that I choose a student to bear that heavy burden of rocks during the lesson.

I had been fully occupied all day with caring for my young children, so I had not had time even to look at the lesson until they were in bed. Scott had been called to the hospital, so here I was, sitting alone at my kitchen table at 9 P.M., struggling to absorb the selected scriptures and other lesson material—and now I needed a backpack and some heavy rocks.

The only backpack in the house was a lime-green baby backpack, the one I'd used to carry my infant children when I was on errands. As for rocks, the largest ones anywhere around the house were no larger than marbles, and I wouldn't leave my children alone to go outside to hunt for bigger rocks. I decided to substitute the next best thing—heavy medical textbooks. We had shelves full of those. I gathered several armloads of heavy books and tossed the canvas backpack on top of them. I was ready for tomorrow's lesson.

As I drove through the dark streets to the seminary, I said another prayer, imploring the Spirit to accompany me during the lesson that day. This scripture ran through my mind as I pulled into the parking lot: "Say nothing but repentance unto this generation; keep my commandments, and assist to bring forth my work, according to my commandments, and you shall be blessed" (D&C 6:9). That thought brought comfort and assurance.

I knew there would be students sitting in my class who would feel instant guilt the moment I announced the topic of the lesson. This was a normal group of Latter-day Saint kids—some of them were struggling with burdens of sin, and others were holding firmly to the "iron rod."

The students gathered (a little late, as usual) for the announcements, surf and weather report (a daily agenda item added especially for this southern California bunch), devotional thought, and opening prayer. When they were quiet and attentive, I began the lesson. I had already chosen the student I wanted to participate in the object lesson: Eric. He had no burdens of guilt of his own. He was an all-American kid: sunny disposition, an Eagle Scout, the oldest of several children, a solid student, a near-perfect specimen of robust health, a kid who loved and respected his parents and wasn't ashamed to say it. I also knew from classroom comments that he felt almost invulnerable to temptation.

Eric came up front and donned the backpack with a grin. I loaded up the backpack with the heavy books, one at a time. The other students watched with interest.

"Are they too heavy?" I asked with every book I added.

"No," Eric declared each time.

Very soon the backpack was filled. I kept handing books to Eric. Each time I asked if his load was too heavy, Eric stubbornly said no.

Finally, Eric held five big books under each arm and carried another eight in the backpack.

"Okay, what do you want me to do now?" Eric asked. "Do I go on a hike?"

"No," I shook my head. "Just stand there. Let me know if you get tired, and I'll relieve you of some of your burden."

"Hey, I'm fine," Eric assured me.

"Okay." I went on with the lesson, all the while keeping an eye on Eric, looking for signs of fatigue. The eyes of all the other class members were glued on Eric, too.

After about eight minutes, I could see Eric's arm muscles twitching.

"Eric, let me take some of those books from you."

"No," he said stubbornly.

In another minute Eric asked if he could sit down and hold the books.

"Sure. You can sit on the corner of the desk, but you can't let the weight of the books rest on the desk. You need to hold them."

"Fine," he said, settling onto the desk, obviously relieved.

Two more minutes went by. I turned to Eric, saw that he was very tired, and asked if he'd like me to remove some of the books.

He shrugged a little, saying, "I guess I wouldn't mind if you took a couple of 'em."

I took one book from each armload.

"Whoa, that feels so much better!" Eric exclaimed.

By now, I was talking about Christ and the gift of the Atonement.

Eric interrupted me, "Hey, if these books are supposed to be sins, I don't want to have to carry them for another second!"

I agreed, pointing out the marvelous parallel of his statement and the reality of carrying the load of sin unnecessarily, when a person could unload his burdens through the process of repentance.

One by one, I relieved Eric of his heavy load of books. Eric told us that the books hadn't seemed very heavy at first, but the longer he held them, the heavier they became.

When I asked him how he felt after the entire load of books had been removed, he said that he felt lighter than air, like he could fly. He stretched and moved his body, exclaiming, "Oh, it feels so good to be able to move again!"

The lessons of this little activity were obvious to all of us. I summarized the process of repentance, urged those who bore their own loads of sin to begin to unload them, bore my testimony of the wondrous gift of the Atonement and my gratitude for the Savior, and then brought class to a close.

As we prayed together before the kids headed out the door for school, I knew I had taught an effective lesson, because I could feel the presence of the Spirit in the room. Saying a private prayer of gratitude before I left the seminary room that morning, I prayed that those students who needed to repent would be motivated to do so.

Frankly, I didn't think again of that particular day's lesson for quite some time.

Two years went by. In that time, Eric moved across the country with his family, graduated from high school, began college, and prepared in earnest for a mission.

We kept in touch. His group of close friends came by my house often, and we sent cassette tapes and pictures back and forth. One sunny day, after hearing Eric brag about surfing in the

Atlantic Ocean, we gathered a crew of my current seminary kids and my own young children and went to the beach to shoot a home movie of the group's best surfing maneuvers. We sent a copy to Eric. It was a smashing success. Eric and his brother filmed and mailed to us their East coast version.

When Eric finished his first year of college, he called me and explained his financial situation. His parents had expected him to raise most of his mission money himself, and he had almost enough. He figured that he could work through the summer and then he'd have enough to be able to file his papers. I offered to send him a small check each month for the duration of his mis-sion—it was all we could spare at the time—and I could hear the joy in his voice when he realized that with that little bit of assis-tance, he could file his papers immediately.

In a month, I heard the terrific news about his mission call. I marked the day on my calendar when Eric would enter the MTC. Carefully timing it, I mailed to the MTC a bright yellow envelope containing my first check and a congratulatory letter.

I was surprised when it was returned to me a week later. Certain that some mistake had been made, I called the MTC office. I was stunned when a kind voice informed me that Eric had not arrived at the MTC.

Frantic, I dialed Eric's number long-distance. It was the middle of the day, but I didn't care. I had to know what had gone wrong. Was Eric ill? Had he been in an accident?

Luckily, Eric's mother was home. When I explained why I was calling, she sounded very weary.

"Annette," she said, her voice heavy with pain, "Eric is all right, but he wasn't able to leave on his mission. That's all I can say right now, but I promise to have him call you, as soon as he can."

I hung up the phone and cried. Something in her voice had

told me that Eric's mission call had been revoked. I decided not to second-guess the reason. I found myself sniffing and choking back tears all through the afternoon. Not Eric. Not this all-American Eagle Scout. Not this golden boy.

Eric did not call that night. I continued to think through the situation and realized that he didn't owe me a call. He certainly owed me no painful explanation. The next afternoon, however, Eric did call. I still recall that conversation.

"Remember that lesson you taught us about repentance," Eric said, "the one when you had me put on a baby carrier and you loaded me up with all those books?"

I remembered.

"Well, I've thought of that lesson a hundred times this month. I've made some pretty big mistakes, and boy, do I feel the weight of them. I know it's going to take a long time, but I'm working really hard to unload these burdens."

It has been years since that conversation. Since then, I've often remembered that lime-green baby backpack and the heaviness of those medical texts. In fact, I've used that object lesson dozens of times in subsequent years, teaching many more teenagers to appreciate the miraculous process of the Atonement that allows us all to cast our burdens upon the Lord.

It took Eric more than a year to get his life back in order. He went through a Church disciplinary council, an excommunication, and a lot of pain and anguish. Many people were affected. After observing the process Eric had to go through, I would never tell anyone that the process of repentance is easy, nor, I am quite certain, would Eric.

Nevertheless, after much prayer, hard work, and repentance, made possible through the miracle of the atonement of Jesus Christ, Eric's Melchizedek Priesthood blessings were restored. Since then, we have shared many momentous occasions, one of which was the day I sent another bright envelope containing a congratulatory note and a little money to the MTC. That time, the letter was answered with a sweet thank-you note penned by Elder Eric.

After a successful mission, Eric courted a mutual friend, a wonderful young woman who had also recently returned from a mission. I felt great joy when these two friends called to tell me they were getting married. Could I be there?

Nothing could stop me. I was in that sacred sealing room to witness the marriage ceremony. The bride was gorgeous. The groom was golden once more.

I have kept a mental picture of that moment tucked in a special corner of my mind. Whenever I've made mistakes, or a friend is weighted down by sin and remorse, I pull out this mental picture. It is a reminder of heavy burdens laid down at the Savior's feet and the miraculous process of change and restoration that we call repentance.

The Wages of Sin

For the wages of sin is death; but the gift of God is eternal
life through Jesus Christ our Lord.
                                    — *Romans 6:23*

"Sister Bowen?"

Even through the phone I could hear the shake in Elizabeth's
voice.

"What is it, Elizabeth?" I asked, hoping she could feel my
love for her.

"I'm pregnant."

As the weight of her words hit me, I dropped down beside
my bed. I said a quick prayer. Help me to say the right thing.
Please help me.

"Oh, Elizabeth, I'm so sorry. How are you feeling?"

"I'm scared to death," she confessed.

"Of course you are. How can I help you?" Dozens of questions
raced through my mind. I asked the most obvious one, "Is Dan
the father?" Dan was a young man who lived just down the street:
a bright, good-looking, soccer player. Dan had recently received
the missionary discussions and been baptized. I adored him.

Elizabeth's voice was a mere whisper. "Yes, Dan's the father."

"Have you talked to him yet?"

Again, the quiet voice, "Yes, I just got through talking with him. He's on a trip with his father, so I had to tell him over the phone. I'm sure he was stunned, but you know how responsible he is . . . he was very kind and supportive. The thing is, neither one of us knows what to do. That's why I called you. I need some advice."

We talked for a long time. I encouraged her to think carefully about her decisions, to read her scriptures and to pray, to counsel with her parents and the bishop. I assured her that she was not alone. Many people loved her and would help her through this confusing and frightening time. I told her how much I loved her and that nothing she could do would alter my feelings for her.

When we hung up, I felt the full effect of Elizabeth's news and wept. These two kids—and that's what they were, *kids!*— had just graduated from high school. They each had great potential and power, bright futures. Elizabeth had been admitted to one of the state's most prestigious colleges. What would happen to that college opportunity? And besides being wonderfully bright, she was also exceptionally beautiful—a homecoming queen, a cheerleader, who was well-liked and well-respected. She should be looking forward to a full life on a college campus, not the terrifying choices she was facing tonight.

And Dan. Dan was a gregarious, happy young man. He was a gifted athlete. He had a tremendous aptitude for mathematics: he had scored in the top two percent on a recent national math aptitude test. He was college bound, as well. Now what?

Dan was a sensitive and responsible young man who had managed to make the most of a tough family situation. When his family had split up when he was in fifth grade, he had chosen to live with his father, "so he wouldn't be lonely."

Never having been exposed to any religious thought, Dan had been attracted to Elizabeth and her beliefs and had investigated the Church on his own. He had a spark of a testimony, but he lived with many questions and a great deal of naivete. I recalled a question he'd asked during a recent lesson about expressing affection in boy-girl relationships, "If you really love someone, why is it wrong to express that love physically?"

Remembering that question, I whispered into the night air, "This is why it's wrong, Dan. This is why." Dan was beginning to learn the lessons of the law of chastity the hard way.

When Dan returned from his trip, he and Elizabeth began the tough decision-making process, as they pondered their future and options. Their parents were sympathetic and supportive, but they left the decisions about the baby and the couple's future to Dan and Elizabeth.

Dan made a list of options, carefully weighing the pros and cons of each. Though he wrote the word down on his list, he quickly realized that abortion was out of the question. At first he leaned toward the option of supporting Elizabeth through the pregnancy and then giving up the child for adoption. Almost immediately, however, he began to wonder about the reality of having his child grow up without him, and he began to question that option as a first choice.

Elizabeth had stronger spiritual roots in the gospel, so she immediately made the decision a matter of prayer. She searched and pondered the scriptures, talked with her parents, and counseled with our bishop. She quickly gained a conviction that she should not give up the baby. The next question for her to consider was whether she should marry Dan. The bishop had asked her to read counsel from the prophet, which encouraged her to marry. Her biggest problem was that she *liked* Dan a lot, but she didn't *love* him. Would those feelings be enough to support a marriage relationship?

Elizabeth asked Heavenly Father if she should marry Dan. She received an unarguable answer. Yes.

She went to Dan. He was willing to marry her, if that's what she wanted. The more he had thought about it, the less he liked the idea of never seeing his child. He had very strong feelings for Elizabeth and believed that they could build a good relationship. He was a relative newcomer to prayers and answers, but he was honestly striving to get an answer. Together, they prayed about a new decision: they would marry and raise this child together. They received the sweet confirmation that this decision was right. It was a particularly wonderful experience for Dan, for now he had his own witness that God hears and answers prayers.

Though many people supported Elizabeth and Dan emotionally, they faced the harsh reality that they had to support themselves financially. They needed to scrape together enough money to rent an apartment, to purchase furnishings and baby supplies, and to pay the hospital bill. They each found two jobs and worked long hours to earn enough money to support themselves and their baby. Elizabeth worked in the office of a builders' supply company during the day; at night, she was a waitress at a steak house. Dan was hired as a bag boy at a local grocery store; he also got a job as a waiter at a restaurant. For both of them, continuing their education was out of the question, at least for a while.

Elizabeth was four months pregnant by the time she and Dan married in October. Their wedding was held in the Relief Society room. It was a simple ceremony, performed by our bishop. It was nothing like the beautiful temple ceremonies I had recently attended. I felt extremely sad and yet hopeful. This young couple was showing great courage, and I admired them for it.

At first, Dan and Elizabeth lived in an extra bedroom at Elizabeth's parents' house, but a wise member of the stake presidency counseled them to get out on their own to build a unified relationship in which they depended on each other.

The only place they could afford was a tiny, one-bedroom, cockroach-infested apartment in an area that bordered on a pretty scary neighborhood. They made the most of it. They were proud of themselves for how hard they worked. They grew to delight in each other's company. Dan, who had always felt lonely as a young boy, discovered that he loved being able to count on Elizabeth's being around. Elizabeth was relieved to feel her heart expanding with affection and, yes, love for Dan.

Together, they worked hard and began to anticipate the arrival of their child. I was impressed by their humility and their willingness to work and sacrifice. And there were many sacrifices: their peers were now in college. Most of Dan's soccer buddies were dating up a storm and enjoying campus life. Elizabeth's friends were enrolled at BYU or Ricks. Only the year before, when she'd been crowned homecoming queen, she had been the envy of every girl in the high school. Now, no one would trade places with her for anything in the world. Still, I'd see Elizabeth's brave smile and watch her gentle acts, I'd enjoy Dan's sunny disposition and hear his positive statements, and my heart would swell with gratitude.

We discussed their plans for the baby's arrival. Elizabeth would have a six-week maternity leave from her office job. When she returned to work, Dan would babysit as much as he could during the day and work at night. He'd been promoted from bag boy to night clerk, and he was very proud of himself.

I felt prompted to offer to care for the baby when they needed help. Elizabeth's mother worked full time, and Dan's mother lived an hour-and-a-half away. They weren't available to help. I discussed the idea with my husband and children, and they all thought it was a great idea. Elizabeth and Dan accepted the offer on condition that when they were making enough money to pay a sitter, they would "let me off the hook." We all agreed.

Brittany arrived in March: healthy, gorgeous, and bald. Elizabeth had all the signs of a nervous first-time mother, but she was determined to be the best mother she could be. From the beginning, there was no question that the baby's needs came first. And Dan! Dan was a proud and delighted father: every move the baby made was a wonder; he showed her off to every person who would stop and look; and he was so tender with her.

The first time I took care of Brittany, after going through Elizabeth's checklist three times and assuring her at least twenty times that we would all be fine, I felt so grateful that Brittany was healthy and whole and that she was being cared for by such loving parents.

"I love your parents, little one," I whispered to her. "They are trying so hard to give you all that you need. They are brave and valiant, and I am so proud of them."

I felt guilty at having the pleasure of baby Brittany in my arms that first morning. I'd seen the look on Elizabeth's face when she turned away from my door and courageously returned to work: she yearned to be able to trade places with me. And yet there was no way that this little family could survive without her income. That was the harsh reality of their situation.

So, morning after weekday morning, Elizabeth or Dan would drive from their tiny apartment south of the city to bring Brittany to me and my boys. Often Dan arrived looking weary after working all night and having had only a little nap in the morning while he cared for Brittany. I worried about him and his health. I couldn't imagine how he managed to get through his long hours of stocking shelves. I wondered how this bright, creative young man survived the tedium and boredom of his job.

The next time Dan came by to pick up Brittany, I asked him about that and about his future plans.

"The job can get very boring, but I'm still very grateful to have it," Dan explained. "It has great health benefits. It pays well. The best thing about it is that the hours are so flexible. Elizabeth and I have discussed it, and we know that I've got to get back in school. If I continue with this job at the store, I can take some classes in the day and work at night."

I was thrilled to hear about his plans to get back in school. "What about Elizabeth?" I asked.

"Her job is quite satisfying and challenging. They really like her, and there is potential for her to earn promotions and pay increases. Our goal for Elizabeth is to get into a situation where she doesn't have to work outside the home. She wants to be home with Brittany. It nearly kills her every time she has to leave for work."

Those were worthy goals: Dan in school, Elizabeth at home with Brittany. They had another goal as well. Following the counsel of their bishop, they were working hard to prepare themselves to go to the temple. They hoped to go be sealed as a family within the year.

The work, effort, and sacrifice that took place in that year's time were incredible. Elizabeth and Dan continued to work hard at their jobs, often without breaks or vacations or adequate sleep. They tried to balance their demanding work schedules with time together, all the while caring for Brittany, who flourished as a result of their constant nurturing. They also struggled through the process of repentance and worked hard to strengthen their testimonies. They filled Church assignments, read books and scriptures, and grew in wisdom and understanding.

One night, Elizabeth stopped by my house with a special request. Their bishop had given them clearance to go to the temple. She smiled, "We want this temple sealing to be the *real* wedding. This time, we want everyone to know that we are marrying each other because we love each other and want to spend the rest of eternity together. We're even having our rings remade so that they can be symbols of this new marriage."

"What a lovely idea!"

Elizabeth beamed. "I have a favor to ask of you."

"What? You know I'll do anything for you."

"When we got married the first time, I was wearing a borrowed dress. This time, I'd like to have my own special temple dress. I can't afford to buy one, but I can afford the material — and I was wondering if you would sew it for me."

"I'd be honored," I replied.

It was a joyful experience for me to sew that temple dress for Elizabeth. She selected a beautiful pattern, and we had fun making adjustments to make it just right. The dress took hours and hours to construct, but I loved working with the beautiful, pure white fabric, which reminded me of the sweet scripture in Isaiah 1:18 that I'd often taught to my seminary students: "Come now, and let us reason together, saith the Lord: though your sins be as scarlet, they shall be as white as snow; though they be red like crimson, they shall be as wool." It was satisfying to watch this promise coming true in Elizabeth's and Dan's lives.

In February, I sat in a beautiful sealing room in the temple with Elizabeth and Dan. The light that shone from their eyes was pure and divine. It was a privilege to observe their sealing to one another. Then little Brittany was brought into the sealing room, dressed in white, with her blonde curls surrounding her little face like a halo. She was placed on the altar, and as her tiny hand rested on her parents' hands, I could see there was not a dry eye in the room. Pure joy. I was intensely proud of Brittany's parents.

I was grateful for their courage, grace, faith, determination, sacrifice, and hard work.

That hard work continued over the next couple of years. Dan registered for a few classes at a local junior college, adding course work to his already crowded schedule. Elizabeth continued working at her office job. They found a regular, paid sitter for Brittany, while attempting to have one of them home with her whenever it was possible.

Their ward was a challenge. Because of the age of the neighborhood, the roster was filled with the names of the elderly. There were few teenagers and even fewer little children. Dan told me that Brittany was the only toddler in the ward. She received a lot of attention, but Dan and Elizabeth struggled to find their place.

Fortunately, a young couple from our ward continued their contact with Dan and Elizabeth. They were both returned missionaries, and they had a child Brittany's age. Their love and friendship were a lifeline for Elizabeth and Dan. Dan told me he was especially grateful for the teaching that took place when the couples were together. He felt that he was lovingly tutored through crash courses in parenting, the plan of salvation, and Melchizedek Priesthood covenants and duties.

Elizabeth became pregnant again. They knew that they would not be able to stay in their apartment when the new baby arrived. They reviewed their budget, wondering how they were going to manage with the expenses of a second child. Dan thought of giving up classes for a while. He hated to do that, though, for he thrived on the challenge of learning. He was also doing very well — so far, he had a 4.0 grade-point average.

One night, Dan and Elizabeth were visiting with friends in our ward, a young attorney who specialized in real estate. He sat down with Elizabeth and Dan and outlined a plan that would enable them to get into a house. Dan and Elizabeth later approached their parents, asking if they might be able to borrow a down payment from them. The parents set up parameters for the loan and agreed to help them.

They searched for an affordable home, finally finding one in a pleasant, family-oriented neighborhood. They investigated the ward and discovered that it was filled with young couples with small children. They were thrilled when their loan was approved, and they moved into the house.

Dan continued working long and hard to support his family. Elizabeth worked in the office of the builders' supply company until the day Daniel, Jr., was born. Her boss offered her a promotion when she returned from maternity leave, but every day that Elizabeth was home with Brittany and little Danny increased her desire to remain at home with them.

Dan and Elizabeth spent hours and hours reviewing their budget, trying to figure out how they could survive without Elizabeth's income. They decided that Elizabeth would have to do something to bring in some money. She considered many ideas and settled on two: she would do what was necessary to get a day-care license, and she would clean houses during hours that Dan could cover their child-care responsibilities.

They hoped these arrangements would be short-term. Elizabeth struggled to care for her own two children as well as five to seven others. Elizabeth learned many tough lessons as she set up the guidelines for her day-care business. A sweet and sensitive young woman, Elizabeth agonized over approaching people who had not paid their child-care bills or people who continually left their children for longer hours than they had contracted. The constant strain of children in her home exhausted her, yet she persevered, knowing that this was the only way she could be with her own children.

It has been eight years since Dan and Elizabeth moved into

their home and started Elizabeth's "temporary" day-care business. Those eight years have been filled with many joys. Dan and Elizabeth now have four beautiful children. When I attended Brittany's baptism two years ago, it was a joy to see a beautiful young girl who had been carefully and prayerfully taught the gospel by her loving parents. Little Danny is preparing for his baptism now.

Elizabeth is a devoted mother—she runs an in-home preschool for her little ones; she schedules a Mom and Me time for each child each week; she has created a beautiful and efficient home for her family and the other children who are fortunate to stay with her. She also serves devotedly in the Church and values the "growth opportunities" she has had.

After eleven long years of labor, sacrifice, and patience, Dan has only one semester left of college. Yes, it's taken him that long to get through school. He still works at the grocery store. He has been offered management positions repeatedly, but he has not accepted them, for with the offers came the responsibility of working six days a week—often on Sundays—and the loss of his flexible work hours, which he has needed in order to meet the emotional needs of his family, to serve valiantly in the Church, and to take college classes.

Has he regretted those decisions? Dan said recently, "You know, I could have moved into management and had a very secure job. But I've been careful not to be seduced by that security, because I do not enjoy the work. I am not happy doing what I do. I've always chosen to take what classes I could toward a degree that will allow me to do what I want to do—something that is challenging, rewarding, and fulfilling. I just didn't ever think that it would take me eleven years to do it. Do I regret those decisions? No. I've been slowly working toward a greater goal."

Eleven years of bagging and stocking groceries is a long time for a young man whose aptitude scores were among the top two percent in the nation. But this young man is also a devoted husband and father (the last time I talked to him, he was at home drawing Little Mermaid characters for decorations for his daughter's birthday party), a bishop's dream of a home teacher, a regular attender at the temple, a kind and loyal friend.

They live with the fact that they mixed up the order of events in their lives, and they regret a choice they made when they were just out of high school. But they are comforted by the balm of peace that they experience, knowing that they have been forgiven. And then there are their children: each of them a gift, each of them a promise.

Dan and Elizabeth would like to help motivate teenagers to obey the law of chastity. To those who find themselves in the frightening position of dealing with a pregnancy, they offer their story as hope. To all of us, they offer their story as proof that Isaiah's sweet promise is true.

They offer their story with love.

"Condemn me not because of mine imperfection; . . . but rather give thanks unto God that he hath made manifest unto you our imperfections, that ye may learn to be more wise than we have been" (Mormon 9:31).

I Believe in You

As thou hast believed, so be it done unto thee.
— Matthew 8:13

I asked a new group of Sunday School students to mark on a list I handed them the lessons they felt they needed. I was surprised by the number of tally marks beside the topic "self-esteem." Almost every person in the room requested lessons on that subject.

I thought specifically of some of the individual self-esteem issues of class members. "I'm so ugly," one girl said repeatedly. That simply was not true. She had beautiful facial features but had not yet figured out the best way to wear her hair or makeup. "I haven't got any talents," one young man had told me. Nonsense. Many times I'd watched him make people laugh and feel at ease in a group. When I asked the students to write one favorite thing about themselves on a piece of paper, several had been seriously stumped, replying, "I can't think of *anything* I like about myself." Although I realized that these statements were teenagers' typical responses, they disturbed me.

If only they could see themselves as God saw them. They seemed not to recognize their innate talents, abilities, and strengths. How could I help them see what I could easily see as

39

I stood in front of them to teach lessons. What beauty in those faces! What promise and potential! What a wonderful mixed bag of personalities, strengths, and weaknesses!

I had no problem preparing the lesson for the first week. As I prayed for guidance, I recalled a memorable lesson activity from my own experience as a seminary student, one that had helped me and had given me strength during my junior year of high school. Thank heaven for that lesson! It proved to be useful still, even all these years later.

One spring day, after we'd gotten to know one another well, my seminary teacher asked us to write our name at the top of a blank piece of paper and then pass it to a neighbor. We then wrote a positive statement about the person whose name appeared at the top of that paper. For the next half-hour, the papers were passed around the room from person to person. It was amazingly easy to write something positive about each person. I was very nervous about getting my piece of paper back, however. Surely, mine would only have a few sentences. What would my fellow students write about me? I was gangly and tall, awkward, loud.

I was shocked when I got my paper back to see that it was full of writing — on both sides of the paper. When class was over I retreated to the girls' rest room to read the comments in private. I couldn't believe how many nice things were written there. Somebody had said I was a natural leader. Another said I was graceful. Me? The "Jolly Green Giant"? Graceful? I was shocked. I kept the paper in my binder for a month and then kept it handy in a drawer by my bed. Whenever I suffered from low self-esteem, I read that paper. It's been twenty years, and I still look at it.

My current class repeated this activity. They hesitated at first but found the task easy once they started writing. I enjoyed watching the smiles creep onto their faces as they wrote. Some had a hard time surrendering the papers when the time came to pass them to the next person — they had more to write! These students had little difficulty recognizing the positive attributes of their fellow classmates, yet when I had asked them to write a list about themselves, they had moaned and groaned and suffered.

The next week, the lesson concentrated on individual gifts and talents. The scriptures yielded wonderful information: we studied Doctrine and Covenants 46, 1 Corinthians 12, and Moroni 10. By the end of the class period, these scripture passages had convinced most of the students that the odds were pretty good that God had blessed them with *something* in the gifts, talents, and strengths division. Just maybe.

The next week, however, I was stumped. I wanted to encourage the students to view themselves in a generous, divine light. I wanted to teach them about believing in themselves and in each other. I wanted to teach them about the power of faith in themselves. How was I going to do that?

As I pondered that problem and prayed about it, I thought of a friend, LouAnn, who has always helped me when I've felt unsure of myself. Whenever I've faced a difficult challenge or assignment, such as the time I had to move across three states while dealing with a physical impairment, or the time I was asked to serve on a community board on drug abuse and felt decidedly unqualified, LouAnn had said, simply, "Oh, Annette, you can do this!"

Those simple words of belief in me and my capabilities were all I needed to get moving. I had a wise, loving friend who believed in me: if LouAnn thought I could do it, then I guessed I could.

Those words, "You can do this!" became a code between us. Back and forth they've flown countless times, a verbal banner of belief and support. Though I've moved a thousand miles away from LouAnn, I still hear her voice when I face a new challenge: "You can do this!" has proved to be self-fulfilling prophecy.

I made a note on the lesson outline to relate that story on

Sunday. Then I saw a small message card sitting on my husband's chest of drawers. I'd left it on the bathroom mirror weeks ago, on a morning when he'd faced a difficult case at the hospital. "I believe in you!" I'd written on a three-by-five card. He'd moved it from the mirror to his dresser, leaving it where he'd see it when he gathered his keys and coins each morning.

"I believe in you!" That's what I wanted my students to know. I believed in them. Their parents believed in them. Best of all, the Lord believed in them and had equipped them with what they needed to succeed. "I believe in you!" were such simple words, but like "You can do this!" they were empowering. I immediately began writing these two statements on small cards. Maybe they'd prove helpful.

That Sunday, I gave each student the two messages, printed on bright-colored, heavy-stock paper. I told the students to put the "You can do this!" card in a prominent place in their rooms and to place the other, "I believe in you!" inside their wallets. That way, every time they opened their wallets or purses, they'd be reminded that no matter what they thought of themselves, someone (many people, actually) believed in them and felt that they could overcome difficulties and succeed.

I did not expect these notes to have immediate effect, but I was wrong.

Two weeks later, on a Saturday morning, I received a phone call from Hillary, a young woman who had recently moved into our ward. Hillary was struggling to make a place for herself in her new surroundings.

"Hi, Sister Bowen. Guess where I am."

I had no idea, but I could hear many voices in the background.

"I'm at the state Distributive Education Clubs of America convention," Hillary declared.

"Good for you! What are you doing there?" I asked.

"Well, last week, my teacher asked if any of us wanted to try out for some of the D.E.C.A. competitions. You know what? Usually, I wouldn't even raise my hand, but then I thought about that little sign you gave us, and I thought to myself, 'Hey, I can do this!' So, I entered two competitions. I *won* one of them and qualified to come to this state convention."

"That's great, Hillary! When is your next competition?" I asked.

"Tonight. That's why I'm calling, so you can wish me luck. I've got that little message card right here in my purse, and I'm going to look at it just before I go up on stage."

Hillary won a medal in the state competition. That success gave her enough fuel to try other new ventures in the following months. She told me several times that the message tucked into her wallet had given her self-esteem a needed boost when she faced difficult situations. "Even though I don't have much faith in myself, it's nice to think that somebody else thinks I'm okay," she told me.

When Hillary left for Brigham Young University (the realization of one of her biggest personal goals), she came to my home to say good-bye. We talked about the challenges that awaited her in Provo.

"You'll be fine, Hillary," I told her. "You can do this."

"Keep telling me that, because I'm scared to death."

"Hey, I believe in you!" I said.

Hillary grinned. "Yeah. I know you do. And I've still got your little message to tell me that. See?" She flipped open her wallet and there was the card, next to her driver's license.

"I'm not the only person who believes in you, Hillary. Lots of people do. I hope you can believe in yourself and the gifts God has given you. And, remember, he'll never abandon you." We hugged long and hard before she left.

Hillary wasn't the only one who told me about the positive power of those cards. Another former student sought me out on his first Sunday home after being away at Ricks College for a year. He opened his wallet to show me the card that declared, "I believe in you!"

"You don't know how many times this card helped me during the year," he said. "I just wanted you to know that it was a good idea. I sure hope you're still giving these cards to your students."

A recently returned missionary, after giving his homecoming talk in our ward, pulled open a very worn wallet to show me a now-tattered, bright-pink slip of paper. "Look!" he said. "I've still got this card. Only I need a new one, next time you make them. I can't tell you how much that little message lifted my spirits when I was down."

"And thus we see that by small means the Lord can bring about great things," Nephi wrote after describing the Liahona and how it worked according to "faith and diligence" (1 Nephi 16:29). The same principles apply as we struggle to see ourselves in divine light. If we have faith in ourselves and in the gifts, abilities, and talents the Lord has given each of us, and if we work with diligence, we will see great things happen.

Over the years I've been privileged to witness many individual victories leading to great events in young people's lives. I now distribute the cards whenever I begin teaching a new group of teenagers. Recently, after distributing these cards to a group of students during a lesson on personal challenges, I shared my private concern about a difficult writing assignment I faced.

One student came up to me after class. "Sister Bowen, you know those little cards you gave us? I think you need to tape one to your desk."

"What a great idea," I said. "Thanks for the suggestion."

"Well, I just think somebody needs to tell you, 'You can do this!' " She flashed a big smile at me as she left the room.

Ah, there were those familiar words, given back to me again in affirmation. Once more, I felt the power inherent in that vote of confidence.

I went home, found one of the bright-pink cards—an extra, left over from my recently taught lesson—and taped it to my computer.

"I believe in you!" The statement that I've sent out to countless young people now greets me every time I sit down at my desk to write.

Becoming

The Lord is my light and my salvation; whom shall I fear? the Lord is the strength of my life; of whom shall I be afraid?
— Psalm 27:1

Jim was an extremely shy fourteen-year-old halfway through an explosive growth spurt and trying to get used to his larger body. He came to our home each month as a silent companion to his father, a devoted home teacher who visited us regularly. Jim probably came reluctantly. During each visit, Jim sat in a corner chair and thumbed through magazines or tinkered with whatever was handy. He answered our questions with a shrug or a simple yes or no whenever we tried to include him in the conversation. He declined all invitations to pray.

It took an earthquake to jar him from silence. We lived in San Diego at the time and occasionally felt tremors from the San Andreas fault. One evening, Jim and his dad were concluding their monthly visit when everything in the house started to shake as the earth beneath our home shuddered. It was the most powerful tremor any of us had ever felt, and was a startling experience. But it was equally startling when Jim started to talk excitedly about what he had felt. I exchanged a look with my husband, "What do you know—he speaks!"

Becoming

Two years later, at sixteen, Jim joined my seminary class. He soon started dropping by my home after school, along with several other students. They would come for fun, haircuts, advice, conversation, and, of course, food. I tried to serve up what they needed. Jim was still the quiet one. In conversation, he had graduated to making short statements, but they were usually succinct one-liners. He wasted no words. He was, however, a comfortable, undemanding kid to have around; and he was well liked by everyone. I came to know him better by observation than by communication.

San Diego is a navy city, and many of the families in our ward, including Jim's, were in the navy. These families moved around a lot, and Jim's family was no exception. Later in that year, Jim's dad received orders to move to Okinawa. Jim struggled with the idea of a move so far away but decided to move overseas with his family. We all said our good-byes regretfully.

Jim didn't write very often, though I wrote to him. One day, however, the mail brought a beautiful cloisonne bracelet for me. There was no card, just a return address: Jim's. His parents also wrote occasionally, so I kept tabs on Jim. I twice received job recommendation requests, so I knew he was working as a lifeguard at the base pool.

The following year, I was surprised one afternoon to open my front door to find Jim standing on my porch. He had flown military standby, along with his sister, to visit friends on the mainland. Most of the other kids were in school or were working, so he spent most of his time at my house — usually by playing quietly with my boys, building Lego structures. He seemed to feel comfortable in our home.

I asked him about Okinawa and his experiences there. He simply answered my questions. I asked about his future plans, and he said he wasn't sure what he was going to do after high school. A few days later, he flew back to Okinawa.

Jim popped up again after he graduated from high school, on his way to Brigham Young University. He showed up a few times more on his way from Utah to California and sometimes to the Far East. I came to expect his unannounced visits. I observed the changes as he grew and matured into a handsome young man. First he grew his hair long and curly, and then he trimmed it back in stages.

He grew up, coming and going through my door. After Jim's nineteenth birthday and a year in Provo, he announced his intention to serve a mission. I was thrilled—but also a little surprised. He had never given me so much as a peek into his soul to share his personal theology. He had never spoken of a testimony. His group of friends was split—some were going in the military, a few were planning on missions, and a few others struggled with individual problems.

Jim went back to Okinawa again, this time to receive a mission call. In a few months' time, he was on my doorstep again, on his way to the Missionary Training Center in Provo. We acknowledged how ironic it was for him to leave the Far East to come to the United States for a mission. During that visit, Jim began to talk. We talked about Japan, about his two dates, about his humorous first kiss, and about his friends and their plans. We discussed his recent trip to the Tokyo Temple to be endowed. We laughed, reminisced, and speculated about our future lives when he returned as an "R.M."

Secretly, I worried about him. How was this quiet, private, young man, who was just now conversing openly after a five-year friendship, going to survive on a mission? I couldn't imagine him tracting, speaking in church meetings, or teaching a discussion. Would he be an ever-silent companion? I prayed for understanding, sensitive, and gregarious companions for him. When his departure day arrived, I sent him off to the MTC with a prayer in my heart for his growth and for his survival.

Jim's letters were few and far between, but they were treasures. In reading his writing, I finally got to know some of his thoughts. He shared some of his feelings and his testimony with me. Mission work was hard. He hoped he could "do the job." He liked some companions and struggled with others. He was always full of faith. His letters proved the adage "Still waters run deep."

Fate and time brought a move for my family and a relocation for Jim's parents. We both moved to the state of Washington. His mother, when we communicated, helped fill in the gaps between Jim's infrequent letters. She gave me news of transfers, of companions, of a new assignment: zone leader. I tried not to be surprised. I matched the depth of the well-written letters with the emergence of this "new" personality who trained elders and taught successful discussions. When his eighteen-month mission neared its end, Jim chose to extend his time for six more months.

On the day that Jim's mission was over, I was privileged to join his family at the airport to welcome him "home" to this place he'd never seen. As I drove to the airport, I reviewed our friendship and Jim's growth and maturation. I speculated about his appearance and his demeanor.

He was the last person to emerge from the jetway, which caused extra anxiety for his awaiting family. Finally, he appeared: taller than I remembered, and thinner. His naturally curly hair was darker and was cut so short that there was no curl. He wore the missionary uniform: dark suit, white shirt, dark tie, black "mailman" shoes. The suit was very worn, and it looked like it could stand on its own and still retain the shape of Jim's body. He was bent a little from the weight of his carry-on luggage.

When he saw us, he smiled a little and then dropped his head as he walked the last few feet of the walkway. When he raised his head again, he was weeping. He seemed to have an aura of light around him. He dropped his bags and embraced his mother in a tight hug, and cried openly as he kissed her, then held her in his arms for a full minute more. He released her to repeat this exchange with his brother, sister, and his father.

It is a rare privilege to observe such an exchange of pure love among people. I thought, This is how it must be to return to our Heavenly Parents after completing our earthly missions. What a sweet experience it must be to return, knowing you've served faithfully, even having gone the extra mile.

Jim then turned to me and without hesitation embraced me in a bear hug. As we parted, we both wiped tears from our eyes. He said, "Thanks for being here."

I thought, by being there, I have recharged my motivational batteries for another seven years. And I am blessed to witness what you have become: a confident, powerful, sensitive, loving man.

I spent another two hours with Jim before we had to go in our different directions. During that time, I watched him start a conversation with the man next to him while they were watching for their luggage to come down the ramp. Within fifteen minutes, he had given the man a Book of Mormon and a pamphlet, and they had parted as friends. I saw him spend a few private, tender moments with his younger brother and sister, focusing on them individually. He gave half of his lunch to his little brother when the ten-year-old complained of still being hungry.

Jim related a few mission experiences: of singing a duet in church with his companion (he sings!); of a Sunday when he had seventeen investigators at church on the same day; and of the mission farewell the night before. Jim's mother told me that half the missionaries had been told to stay put by the mission president, or they all would have been there. Jim seemed puzzled that so many missionaries wanted to say good-bye to him, and he explained it by saying, "The missionaries really love each other."

And they especially love you, I thought.

Jim wept again as he expressed his concern for a companion who had recently lost his dad — it was a sudden, unexpected death. I wept, too. Here was compassion. Charity. Pure love. Humility. Confidence. And power.

Sitting before me, in his grayed shirt, wrinkled tie, and well-worn coat (the lining was in strings), was someone who had been transformed. His smile was the only trace of the shy, quiet kid who had declined to pray in front of someone.

We send our young men and young women, our sons and daughters, our brothers and sisters, and our students and friends out to preach the gospel of Jesus Christ. We ask them to study, to work hard, to endure, and to go out to serve God and his children. Most of these children return to us whole, ready to teach and inspire by their loving and humble example. And, having been touched by divine light, we are, none of us, the same again.

Write It!

For we labor diligently to write, to persuade our children, and also our brethren, to believe in Christ, and to be reconciled to God.
— *2 Nephi 25:23*

I believe in the power of the written word.

I have a great love for the writings in the scriptures. My heart and mind have often been moved by these records of ancient prophets and peoples. Their words bridge the centuries, and they reach out to touch and teach me.

I have also had a longtime love for great literature. I have been moved, taught, and influenced by many fine writers, including authors of classics — Tolstoy, Chekhov, Eliot, Hardy, Austen — as well as contemporary writers — Steinbeck, Cather, Hemingway, O'Connor, Olsen, Dillard. My life would be bleak without their books.

I've learned that the writing process itself is therapeutic. For years, I've taught classes on journal writing. I don't believe I've ever taught a class without hearing some variation of these comments: "When something is wrong, I sit down and write about it, and then I feel much better"; or, "You know, when I don't think I've accomplished anything in my life, or made any progress, then I read my journal, and I see that I'm wrong"; or, "My journal reminds me of personal victories." My own journals have expanded to more than two thousand pages. They are among my most precious possessions.

I also know that the written word often has the power to communicate tender feelings, to heal, and to touch people who are seemingly out of reach. Often the written word can succeed when spoken words have failed.

Aaron was a student whose name was printed on the roll. Unfortunately, I rarely saw him. Week after week I marked him absent from Sunday School.

Aaron's family puzzled me. They were a strong family, devoted to family unity. I knew Aaron's mother had a testimony of the gospel, yet the family attended church only sporadically. Aaron attended even less frequently than the other members of his family did.

Usually, in a "case of a missing student," I would talk to the parents and offer assistance, if they desired it. But I didn't want to offend Aaron's parents by mentioning that I didn't see their child (or them) at church very often. Instead, I asked a few of the kids at church about Aaron. "He's a loner," I was told. "Good luck with him. He's always been like this." They didn't sound encouraging.

One morning, while writing some letters, I thought about my friend Karla. Her family had been totally inactive in the church. Then her son, Luke (who is now a returned missionary), began receiving notes and calls from a dedicated and persistent Primary teacher. Karla finally decided she'd better take Luke to Primary to meet this person. She and Luke quickly returned to activity in the Church and have been devoted members ever since.

Maybe I should write a little note to Aaron, I thought. What did I have to lose? Surely his curiosity would compel him to open the note and read it. Maybe I'd even luck out and touch a responsive chord. I wrote something like this:

"Dear Aaron,

"You're on my mind this morning, so I decided to write you a note.

"I hope everything is all right with you.

"If you ever need a friend, I'm available.

"Love,

"Annette Bowen

"P. S. I miss seeing you in Sunday School class."

I immediately walked to the mailbox with the note, in case I changed my mind.

The next Sunday, I went to my classroom to prepare it for the lesson. I was more than a little surprised to find Aaron waiting there for me.

"Hi. I got your note," he said simply.

"So, how are you?" I asked.

"Actually, I'm not too good at the moment," he replied.

"Can I help?"

"Maybe. We'll see."

At that moment, a group of students burst into the room, ending our conversation.

The next week, Aaron was again waiting when I arrived in the classroom. This time, after the lesson, he stayed to talk to me about a problem.

He didn't come the next week, but he came the next. Again, he was waiting for me when I entered the room.

That became our weekly routine: Aaron would come most Sundays. He'd be in the room before I arrived. We'd have two to five minutes of private conversation before the other students entered the room. If he needed to talk longer, he'd wait after class.

Those short conversations led to longer ones. Occasionally, he'd phone my house to talk. Sometimes he'd drop by. One day, he treated me to one of his beautiful music compositions. I'd heard that he played the piano, but I'd also heard that he usually wouldn't play for an audience. I was touched by his gift to me, when he sat at my piano and played. He was an extremely talented musician.

Eventually, Aaron turned eighteen and decided to attend our stake's young adult branch. Before he left, he paid me a final, before-class visit. "I hope you don't mind my leaving," he said, "but I think I've outgrown this group."

"Of course I mind," I teased. "I'm going to miss our chats. But I understand you need to move on, so I'll make the sacrifice."

He smiled. "We'll still be friends."

Yes, we'll still be friends, I thought — all because I once wrote one little note expressing concern and offering friendship.

Another story. Kim and Holly had been best friends since Holly moved into the ward earlier in the year. They were drawn to each other immediately and soon shared lunches, after-school hours, confidences, and dreams. In February, Kim did something that hurt Holly's feelings, and Holly retaliated. That exchange soon escalated to an all-out war. Both of them had hurt feelings. Both of them felt betrayed. Both of them, though they professed not to care anymore, secretly wished that they could resolve their differences and be friends again.

I listened to both of them. Each poured out her frustrations, along with some tears. I felt I was walking a tightrope and told them so. They wanted advice, and I carefully doled some out: be nice, be forgiving, render some service to each other. Still, the war raged on, and began to spread. Soon, many of the teenagers in the ward were taking sides.

Holly came to me again. "This is getting ridiculous!" she

declared. "Kim's been in this ward forever, and everyone is on her side. She's the one who did something wrong in the first place!" she cried. "Now I don't have any friends."

Together, we reviewed Holly's options. None were attractive to her. Finally, exasperated, I asked her, "Can't you just send her a card and say, 'This has gotten out of hand. I miss you. I'm sorry.'?"

Holly sat in silence. Finally, the corners of her mouth turned up a little, and she asked, "Do I *have* to apologize?"

"I think it would be a very good idea," I replied.

"Well, maybe I can do that. Tell me the words again, and I'll write them down. I'll use my break at work to find a good card about friends, and then I'll give it to Kim. Maybe it will work."

Holly bought the card the next day and delivered it herself. She called me that night.

"How did it go?" I asked.

"It was awful."

"You're kidding!" I was stunned. "What went wrong?"

"Well, I took the card to where Kim works, and I handed it to her. She opened it on the spot and read what I wrote. Then, get this. She looks at me and says, 'Apology accepted.' That was it. She didn't say that she was sorry, or that she still wanted to be friends, or anything. Now I'm madder than ever. She's the one who started this whole thing, and she owes me an apology!" Holly was irate.

"Well, you've done what you could," I said, "and I'm proud of you for doing it."

"Big deal," she said. "That still leaves me without a friend."

I hung up, heavyhearted. I admit I was also a little miffed at Kim. I debated calling her but decided I'd better let the two of them handle it.

Several weeks later, Kim stayed after class. "Sister Bowen, have you got a minute?"

"Sure."

"Can I talk to you about Holly and me?"

"You bet," I said. I gathered up my lesson materials, and we went to a private corner of the building.

"Tell me what's on your mind," I said.

Tears pooled in Kim's eyes, and she poured out her sad side of the story. I heard about some of the things Holly had done and said (things that Holly had not told me), which reminded me that, especially in relationships, there are always two sides to any story.

Then Kim told me about Holly's card. It had really touched her. "I don't know what got into me that night," she moaned. "But, by that time, Holly had really hurt me and I figured she did owe me an apology, so I told her that I accepted her apology. I was going to tell her that I really missed her and wanted to save our friendship, too, but Holly didn't give me a chance. She turned around and almost ran out of the store, so I didn't get to finish what I was saying."

Kim and I reviewed her options.

"You two really need to sit down and talk this thing out," I told her. "I suggest that you meet at some neutral territory, like a park, and allow yourselves a lot of time to talk it out. Tell Holly the things you're telling me. Then allow her to tell you her side of this whole thing."

"I don't think I can do that," Kim said, shaking her head.

"Why?"

"Because we'll just get in a bigger fight. She's a better talker than I am, and whenever I say anything, she pounces on it and runs away with it. I don't think we could have a real discussion. I think it would make things worse."

"Then, can you write to her and tell her what you're thinking and feeling?"

"I don't think she'd read anything I wrote."

"Kim," I said, "have you ever received a personal letter that you haven't read?"

"No," she admitted.

"Neither have I," I said. "If you write Holly a letter, she'll read it."

"But what would I say, if I wrote this letter?"

"All of the things that you're telling me. Tell her that you're sorry. Apologize for the things you've done. Tell her that the things she's done have hurt you, but that you want to put them aside. Tell her that you treasure her friendship and want to have it back."

"Do I write all of that?"

"Sure. The best thing about writing it is that you can write several drafts if you need to. You can rewrite the letter until it's just the way you want it, and you can say all of those sensitive, hard-to-say-out-loud kinds of things."

Kim thought about it. She nodded her head a little. "I think I can do that." Then she smiled. "You know what the best thing is about this plan?"

"What?"

"Holly can't argue back."

I laughed. "Nope, at least not until she's read every word you've written, and by then, I don't think she'll feel like arguing."

Kim hugged me. "Thanks, Sister Bowen, I think this might work."

I prayed that it would.

Kim wrote a long letter to Holly. She brought me her final draft and asked me to make sure she had said all the things we'd talked about. It was a beautiful letter.

Holly called me the next afternoon. "Hi, Sister Bowen. Guess what happened today?"

"What?"

"Kim wrote me a long letter and gave it to me at school. She actually apologized! She says that she misses me and wants for us to be friends again."

"How do you feel about it?"

"I feel great! I think everything's going to be just fine."

"Is it that simple?"

"Sure it's that simple," Holly said.

I knew that it wouldn't really be that simple to salvage the friendship. But at least they had made a start.

"Hey, you know what else?" Holly said. "She said that my card really touched her. She's thought a lot about it, and that's what inspired her to give me her letter. I guess this writing business really does work."

I agreed. This writing business really does work. For Kim and Holly, the written word had bridged an enormous gap and paved the way for a new building phase of their friendship.

A final story. By the time my students graduate from high school, I've usually known them for two or more years. After that much time, the name of each of My Kids has been inscribed indelibly across my heart. As I've faced one June after another, I've expressed this love in a letter, privately and individually, to each of my students before he or she graduates from high school and moves on. These letters have provided the opportunity for me to thank each beloved friend for some of the lessons or experiences we've shared and to articulate my hopes and dreams for each individual. At the end of each letter, I've written my name, phone number, and address, along with my wish to hear from him or her over the years.

I've written these letters because of two letters I received when I was a senior in high school.

The first one arrived at my home in early spring. My name and address were written in beautiful script on an envelope of cream-colored vellum. Inside, I discovered a beautiful sheet of stationery bearing a floral design of burgundy roses. It was perfumed. This was the message, written in the same fluid script I'd noticed on the envelope:

"Annette dear,

"You are a joy to me, and I love having you in fourth period!

"How lucky I am that you moved to Reno.

"Thank you for everything.

"With love,

"Margaret Muth"

I was touched by that simple, generous gesture. I'd never received a letter from a teacher before. I had struggled during that year, trying to meet the many new challenges that resulted from my family's moving from another state a week before my senior year began. It had not been easy. I'd often felt that I didn't have a friend in the world. Then, this lovely letter arrived, and it marked a turning point for me. I saved the letter, and read it many times.

A few months later, just before graduation, I received another note from Mrs. Muth. Again the message was succinct but generous:

"Knowing and loving you has helped me be a better person and teacher." It was another note to save and treasure. I still have these two letters.

Mrs. Muth was my senior English teacher. She was the most powerful teacher I'd ever had. I knew she had influenced me greatly that year, but I had no idea at that time how long I would feel her influence. It has spanned my adult life. Every time I write a story or an essay, I find myself answering to Mrs. Muth's tough demands and high expectations. She died shortly after she wrote me those sweet letters. You may have noticed that this book is dedicated to her memory.

Now I send my students off to their adult lives with a personal letter.

Not long ago, a former student reentered my life, the result of one of those letters. I had not heard from Patrick in years. In fact, I had no idea where he was. I knew he had joined the armed services after graduating from high school and that he worked in intelligence. I'd received a wedding invitation from him some years later and knew that he'd married outside the Church. In response to the invitation, I had sent a gift and a note, but I hadn't heard from him since.

Five more years passed, and then, one day, I discovered Patrick's still-familiar handwriting on an envelope in the mail. Smiling, I carried the envelope to my favorite chair and opened it.

Patrick had written two pages of news: he was going through a special language school. He had risen through the ranks. He and his wife had two sons, and they were expecting another child soon. I savored every word.

On the third page, Patrick wrote about the struggles he was having in his marriage. His wife hated the Church. Because of her attitude, in an effort to save his marriage, he had stopped attending, but he missed it terribly and wondered what he could do. He felt that he faced a difficult decision: his marriage or his church? Could I call him or write to him?

That evening I dialed the number he had printed at the end of the letter.

Patrick told me, "I don't know if you remember this or not, but before I graduated, you wrote me a letter. I've saved that letter, and it gave me the courage to write to you now. You asked me to keep in touch and said that I could contact you if I ever had a problem. Well, I have one."

We talked about his struggles in an unhappy marriage and the difficult choices he faced. I encouraged him to turn to the Lord and to seek counsel with his bishop.

Since then, Patrick and I have talked many times. How blessed I feel to have him as a friend.

Recently, during another long-distance call, Patrick asked me, "Are you still teaching teenagers?"

I chuckled. "Yes, I am."

"Well, will you do me a favor?" Patrick asked. "Will you tell them that you have a former student who didn't listen to the lessons about marrying in the Church and in the temple, and as a result, his life is a huge mess? I'm serious about this. Will you tell them? Tell them to listen to those lessons, because they're very important. Right now, it would be really great to think that somebody could learn from my mistakes. If I could spare one kid from making the mistakes I've made—from living with this kind of pain—I would feel a whole lot better."

The next Sunday, I told my class Patrick's story and gave them his message.

I felt that I needed to write about it, as well. Maybe Patrick's words, recorded here for others' benefit, will have the power to help someone.

"These are written, that ye might believe" (John 20:31).

Holding the Rod

*To stand as witnesses of God at all times and in all
things, and in all places . . .*
      — Mosiah 18:9

Several years ago, in teaching a Sunday School class of twenty
high school juniors and seniors, I had a unique challenge. In this
class were exemplary young men — the kind of young men who
are a mission president's dream. Teaching them and loving them
was a treat. Along with these young men, however, was a group
of young women unlike any I'd ever encountered — they were a
Laurel teacher's nightmare. Teaching them and loving them was
like running an obstacle course: they wanted to see how high I
could jump, how fast, and how far. They put me through my paces
regularly, testing my love and endurance.

Fortunately, I was not alone in that race. My husband was
the bishop, and a dear friend was the Young Women's president.
Together, we did the best we could at loving, listening to, and
directing these young women while wearing out the carpet beside
our beds praying for guidance and direction.

In the midst of this group of Laurels were two girls of strength,
faith, integrity, and tranquility: Alison and Anne. The thought of
them still makes me smile. They were the calm center in the
storm of that year.

Alison and Anne shared a most unusual relationship: they were teenaged sisters who actually liked each other. They drew strength from each other and from a wonderfully strong family— I could sense the bond between them when they spoke kindly to each other, or shared a laugh, or continually included the other sister in plans. Alison and Anne were blessed with physical beauty, but their inner beauty was far greater even than their pretty faces. Their countenances radiated light. They were talented. They were hard workers. They were responsible. They were the kind of young women that parents, teachers, and Church leaders want to clone.

Being beautiful, wholesome young women, Alison and Anne attracted the attention of the exemplary young men in the class, who vied for their special friendship. A young man would make his move at a youth activity or dance. Balloons, cards, and flowers would follow. Then, at some point, a rather downcast young man would tell me, "She [meaning Alison or Anne] just wants to be friends." The word *friends* was pronounced as if it were the saddest word in the English language. "She says she doesn't want to get into a serious relationship. She says she's not ready for that yet."

Good for her! I'd say to myself. These girls were beautiful, friendly, talented. And smart.

Now, you'd think that these sisters would pull away from the other girls in their age group or that the other young women would reject them, jealously, for being too wonderful. You'd think Alison and Anne would get tired of the antics, turmoil, and trouble that followed the others like dust clouds behind a truck on a country road. You'd think that Alison and Anne would want to shrug off the responsibility of being friends to them.

But they didn't. They took seriously the challenges and stewardship of serving as class officers as well as the Lord's admonition to love one another. They were kind. They were accepting and nonjudgmental. The other teenagers (even the other young women) liked having them around.

On a Friday night, I'd see them — all of them — at the video store, as a group, selecting movies for the night's entertainment. Some afternoons, I'd pass them, piled into a car on the main street by the high school after school was over for the day. At church, they would congregate in the hall to laugh and visit.

On more than one occasion, before my class was to begin, I'd hear either Alison or Anne say, "Come on, you guys. Let's get to class." They'd head down the hall, and the rest of the group would follow. Now, I know why the boys followed, but I have no doubt that the other girls would have happily stayed in the foyer for the duration of Sunday School, or, better still, gone to the nearby doughnut shop. Instead, they followed Alison and Anne into class.

Alison and Anne were the kind of friends that parents and teachers refer to as "good influences." I often wondered how many videos were left on the shelf as Alison or Anne would say, "No, I don't think so. How about this one?" as they held up a better alternative. Or how many other inappropriate activities were quietly but firmly censored in favor of something more wholesome.

I know Alison and Anne worried and fretted about their troubled (and troublesome) friends, because they told me of their concerns for them and for the choices their friends were making, often with eyes brimming with tears and voices quivering as they spoke.

I worried about Alison and Anne. How could they continue these associations and not be negatively affected? How did they survive the emotional upheavals? How were they going to stay on the right and true course with such diversion going on around them?

When I expressed my concern to Alison and Anne, they each shared the same survival tactics. They were very simple, really: they just stood their ground and didn't compromise their principles. They took a stand. They held to the iron rod.

As a result of their stand, when Alison and Anne were around, language would get cleaned up, activity plans would be changed, and secret acts of service were rendered.

Alison and Anne made a difference in their friends' lives. One of the other Laurels told me that she'd obviously made many mistakes, but she was always a better person when she was around those two young women. She laughed as she said, sarcastically, "I don't want to corrupt them," but she meant what she said. Though she found plenty of trouble on her own, I wonder how much trouble she avoided by simply being with Alison and Anne.

Alison and Anne are now away at school. They work part-time jobs to help support themselves. They serve in callings in their wards. They are conscientious students. They share their talents freely. No, they are not perfect, but they continue to walk the path of truth and light: they are still holding to the rod. I am sure, when they are tried or tested, they continue to apply their simple solution: they quietly but firmly take a stand for what is right. And, of course, they have each other and their strong family bonds to lend support.

At Christmastime each year, the young people from our ward who have been away at school, in the service, or on missions speak to us in sacrament meeting to tell us what they've experienced and learned. During their first Christmas home from college, both Alison and Anne spoke. Their faces were radiant with increased light, and their words were powerful as they told of increased knowledge. They thanked ward members for teaching them and supporting them, and then they bore sweet testimonies of love for their family and for their Lord and Savior, Jesus Christ.

I never think about what I might have taught them. I think, instead, of what Alison and Anne have taught me. Their names will always make me smile at the memory of two sisters who liked each other; who day by day, day in and day out, not only listened but believed—and being believers, held to the rod and quietly, repeatedly, took a stand for righteousness.

I still associate Alison's and Anne's names with the strength, integrity, and tranquility that I observed during that tumultuous time, but now I also recognize their pervasive good influence and gentle power.

And I still want to clone them.

Patience

And the servant of the Lord must not strive; but be gentle unto all men, apt to teach, patient, in meekness instructing those that oppose themselves.
— 2 Timothy 2:23–24

I wondered about Greg. He puzzled me. He seemed to resent being in seminary every morning, yet, he kept appearing, morning after morning. Why did he attend?

Greg's family had recently converted from Catholicism. His parents had tender testimonies of the gospel and were eager to be fully active in the Church, but it seemed that Greg had not experienced a change of heart. I surmised he was not inwardly motivated to attend early-morning seminary but attended simply because his parents expected him to.

He didn't attend happily, however. He'd arrive late each day, many times in the second half of the hour. He'd shuffle to a seat on the back row, toss his books down on the floor or the desk, and then glare at me, inviting a reaction.

I didn't give him one. I was thrilled that he showed up at all. So, day after day, when he pushed through the door, I'd give him my most generous smile and a cheerful, "Good morning, Greg." Then, ignoring his noise, I'd let him settle in his back seat and go on with the lesson.

Patience

After his late arrivals, Greg talked and laughed with Brent, another back-row regular; sometimes he'd manufacture spitwads by the dozens, sending them forward into the backs of the other students. Other students goofed around from time to time, as well, but at least they'd make an effort to participate in class. And much of the time they actually seemed to be listening.

Greg sent the message loud and clear that he did not wish to participate in class. He usually busied himself with last-minute homework, or doodled, or slumped down in his chair to sleep. He refused to pray. When I asked him a question, he'd mumble, "I dunno," or make some supposedly humorous remark. I tried every trick in the book to draw him into discussions and lesson activities, but he stubbornly refused.

Stubborn. That's the word that best described Greg. He was strong-willed. He liked to do what he wanted to do. He didn't want to be "encouraged." To force him to do something was completely out of the question.

I prayed about Greg. A lot. I couldn't figure out why he kept showing up, morning after morning, when he obviously detested the whole idea of seminary, and I certainly did not want to give him any reason to stop coming to class; however, I also wanted him to learn something. How could I reach him? Could I help him with his anger? What could I do to engage his interest in scripture study and class discussions? I reviewed teaching manuals, conferred with my supervisor, and searched the scriptures. Finally, I decided just to let Greg be.

Greg continued to wage a cold war against me. My only response was to exercise patience and to try to show him, and my other students, enough warmth and love eventually to melt his icy stare.

Day after day, week after week, month after month, Greg continued his back-row routine of arriving late, throwing spitballs, making occasional smart-aleck remarks, catching up on home-work or sleep, or doodling. I continued to greet him cheerfully, smile, invite him to participate, and work hard on my lessons, hoping that he'd hear something useful, if he ever tuned in. I doubted that he did.

One day, after I'd distributed a worksheet to the students, I wandered from desk to desk, answering questions, checking on the students' work. I glanced at the back row and was not surprised to see Brent folding the worksheet into a sleek paper airplane nor to find Greg doodling on the back of the worksheet.

I wanted them to know that I was no fool, that I knew they weren't working. "How are you guys doing back there?" I asked.

"Just fine," Brent gleefully answered, as he sent his paper airplane soaring toward me.

Greg mumbled something I couldn't hear.

I went back to my desk, grabbed two more worksheets, and did some muttering of my own. What I really wanted to do was to march back there and wring their necks or at least tell them how tired I was of their antics and how much I'd appreciate a little support from them. Far from confirming that feeling, the Spirit whispered, "Be patient."

Instead of marching back intent on wringing their necks, I calmly walked toward them with the replacement worksheets. "Hey, guys, come on. These worksheets aren't that bad. Look, it's a crossword puzzle. It might be fun. See how much you can do. I'm available, if you get stumped."

I handed Brent the paper. He shrugged, pulled out a pencil, and pretended to think about the puzzle. Experience had taught me that at the end of class the paper would still be blank, but I was willing to settle for some peace in the classroom, so I left him in his silent "thinking" and turned to Greg.

Greg looked up at me, and what I saw on his face surprised

me. I didn't see anger. I didn't see belligerence. What I saw was a face set with determination, ready for a challenge. But his eyes were pleading, "Don't be angry with me. Please just accept me."

Before saying a word, I looked down at Greg's paper and was startled by what I saw there. He had been doodling on the back of the puzzle, all right. But this was no formless scribbling. This was a carefully designed and executed monogram, complete with fleurs-de-lis and curlicues surrounding painstakingly formed, elaborate letters. It was beautiful work.

The name on the paper was mine.

"Greg," I whispered. "This is gorgeous! I didn't know you could draw like this."

He shrugged, but his eyes met mine. There was still a plea in them, "Please like me. Please like my work."

"Do you always doodle like this?" I asked.

"Sometimes," he mumbled. "I do a lot of drawing."

"Do you take an art class at school?"

"Yeah. I do some commercial artwork through a vocational class." He was still muttering, but I thought I could detect a little healthy pride hiding in his statement.

"I'd like to see more of your work. Do you have anything else with you?"

"Not really. But you can see some of my ad work in the yellow inserts in Thursday's paper. I drew some of the sale items."

I was genuinely surprised. "Which ones?"

Greg told me which store ad to look for and which tools he'd drawn. I promised to look for them.

I wanted to ask for the monogram, but I didn't dare. We'd finally had a nice conversation, and I didn't want to push things. Deciding to let him off the hook, I didn't give him another copy of the crossword puzzle. It was time to conclude the lesson, anyway.

After the closing prayer, the students gathered their books, backpacks, and bags and headed out the door to school. Usually, Greg was one of the first to shoot out the door, but today, he lingered. I walked to the back row.

He'd left the monogram on the desktop.

"You want that?" he asked, when he saw me look at it.

"I'd love it," I replied, and picked up the paper from the desk.

"It's not very good. It's kind of lopsided. I can do a better one for you, if you want."

"No, I'd like to have this one. It's lovely. I'd like to hang it on my bulletin board at home."

"Well, then, you can keep it," Greg said.

"Thank you. I'd like to see more of your doodles sometime. Will you show me some?"

"Sure." He almost smiled, but he caught himself.

"Well, Greg, if you do work like this, you can doodle all you want in here," I said. "Be my guest."

"That's what I'm doing back here most of the time. I know you think I don't listen, but I do. I hear a lot of what you're saying. I just don't want to talk or pray or anything."

"That's okay. I understand. I won't ask you."

With that guarantee, Greg was out the door, leaving me holding his lovely work, a combination tribute and trophy.

From that day on, Greg and I had a truce. Yes, he still came in late; yes, he still slumped into a seat on the back row; and yes, he still whispered and laughed with Brent, his back-row partner.

I overlooked his behavior. I was happy to see Greg come through that door each day, no matter how late, for sooner or later, he'd pull out a clean piece of paper and a pencil and commence with his marvelous doodles. And though I had never suspected it, I knew now that as he doodled, he also listened.

In the months that followed, Greg and I became better friends.

He always held himself back, maintaining the distance between us that the other students had long ago surrendered, but he occasionally shared some of his artwork with me or came to a gathering at my house and hung around the periphery.

Greg's family moved away the next year. I wrote him a long letter before he left and asked him to keep in touch with me.

I was surprised when he did.

It's been nearly ten years since then, but, through them all, I've had letters and postcards from Greg, written in an artistic, fluid hand. The letters have been treasures, revealing a sensitive, intelligent Greg who struggled for truth. Better than the letters, however, have been the occasional long-distance phone calls and the personal visits, always surprises.

The last time I saw Greg, he had made a special visit to my home to introduce me to his bride. They were on their honeymoon, yet they made time to drop by my house for an afternoon.

During our conversation, Greg turned to his wife, and said, "You can't believe what Sister Bowen put up with when she was our seminary teacher."

"I can imagine," Laura groaned.

"Oh, come on, Greg. You guys weren't that bad," I replied.

"Yes, we were. Brent and I were terrible. We'd sit on that back row, trying to upset you; but no matter what we did, you'd never get upset. You must've had the patience of Job."

Patience. I treasured his statement, for patience has never been one of my stronger virtues. I thought back to that year. I had been scared, frustrated, and perplexed. I hadn't had a clue what to do with Greg, except to love him. After much prayer and pondering, I had settled for the happy fact that he was, at least, slumped in a chair in a seminary class each morning, even if he wasn't participating.

I thought, too, of the many times the Spirit had restrained

me from locking horns with him or answering his challenges. That restraint, or "patience," combined with my determination not to give Greg a reason to leave seminary, had worked. He'd kept coming.

"Did that year make any difference in your life, Greg?"

"Of course it did. You have no idea."

Now was my chance to ask Greg the question I'd always wanted to ask. "Greg, tell me something. Why did you go to seminary? I didn't think you liked being there at all."

Greg laughed. "At first, I hated being there. I hated getting up that early. I hated hearing all that scripture stuff. My parents had joined this new church, and I felt like everybody was stuffing it down my throat. You know me, I'm stubborn and strong-willed. I didn't like it at all."

"So, your parents made you come?"

"Yeah, I guess you could say that. Mom woke me up each morning and tried to coax me out of bed. But that wasn't always enough to get me going. So, they went to something that would be a better motivator: they hooked my car privileges to my seminary attendance."

"You went to seminary so that you could drive?" I asked.

"Yeah. I came so that I could drive," Greg admitted. "But I think I ended up driving you crazy."

"Hardly," I responded.

Greg turned to Laura, "I'd come late. I'd make a lot of noise coming in. Brent and I were nothing but trouble. But no matter what we did, she'd just smile at us and take it. I was itching to have a confrontation. I was trying to give her a reason to kick me out. I wanted to be kicked out, so I could blow up and never have to come back. But she never reacted the way I wanted her to. And, eventually, I gave up, and started to listen. After that, slowly, things began to make sense."

Turning to me, he said, "You know the rest of the story."

Yes, I knew the rest of the story: it included many moves with his family; a struggle to obtain his own testimony of the gospel; a year of commercial art school; a decision to serve a mission; a year spent working full-time to earn mission money; a tough, challenging mission in France; another move; enrollment in college; more hard work; the courtship of a lovely nursing student met at a church dance; and now a marriage in the temple.

I liked the story.

In the years since Greg issued my first big challenge as a seminary teacher, I've encountered many more students like him. They come in various shapes and sizes. They are girls and guys. Sometimes they don't come in to class at all and have to be coaxed in from hallways or pulled into participation by friends.

When they do come in, they still sit on the back row. They still throw spitwads and fold paper airplanes. They still laugh at private jokes and make caustic remarks. They still declare private cold wars, or they wear defiant masks. They all seem to be daring me to teach them something.

I'm still glad they're there. I no longer wonder what to do with them: I just love them. I welcome them, accept them, and try to include them in whatever is going on. I've learned a little in the patience category over the years.

One more thing I've learned: sometimes it takes a long time for a student to hear and then to act on what he or she has heard. Often, years pass before you get to hear the best parts of a student's story. The apostle Paul knew what he was writing about when he shared his words of wisdom about teaching and gentleness and patience. They work.

Pray Always

But behold, I say unto you that ye must pray always, and not faint; that ye must not perform any thing unto the Lord save in the first place ye shall pray unto the Father in the name of Christ.
— 2 Nephi 32:9

Brooke had been frustrated and depressed for a long time, though she admitted it to only a few people. If someone asked how she was doing, she'd say, "Fine!" She was an excellent actress, and most people she associated with considered her to be a capable, happy person.

Because we'd become good friends, I knew that beneath Brooke's bravado was a person who had struggled for a long time with low self-esteem. Somehow, no matter what she accomplished or how many friends she had, she couldn't feel really accepted and loved.

Forget that her parents adored her and would do anything to support her. Forget that she was almost constantly surrounded by friends. Forget that she knew that God loved everybody: she was certain that she was excluded from his love. Besides, she told me, her friends hung around only because she had a car; and her parents supported her only because they had to.

I wondered why Brooke seemed unable to accept the love

that was around her. After many months and many conversations, I finally discovered the "missing puzzle piece": Brooke had made some mistakes in the past and had not worked through the repentance process. She was carrying around a load of "Dumb Things I've Done" and had not figured out how to drop it.

Living with this load, Brooke had convinced herself that no one around her would love her "if they really knew her." Her parents wouldn't accept her. Her friends would abandon her. God already hated her, of course, because he did know.

Another of Brooke's confidants and I teamed up to nudge her toward her bishop. Brooke seemed unable to resolve her issues on her own through prayer, so we thought maybe it would help for her to talk to him.

It helped some. He counseled with her and tried to convince her that no matter what she'd done, Heavenly Father loved her, still; and that she needed to forgive herself so that she could move forward, instead of clinging to these mistakes in her past.

Brooke soon went away to college. Knowing that she still struggled with depression and low self-esteem, I exacted a promise from her that she would write or occasionally call.

Through her letters, I learned that Brooke was struggling to obtain a testimony that God truly existed and that he loved her.

During a telephone call, she told me, "I don't get it. I'm doing everything I can, but I still don't have a testimony. I go to church and listen to the other kids, and it seems like everybody's figured this out but me. What's the problem?"

"Are you praying?" I asked.

"Yeah, but nothing ever happens, so I've about given up."

"Don't give up!" I pleaded with her. "You need to keep praying." I knew she was fairly impatient. "Can you try to operate on faith for a while and keep saying daily prayers?" I asked.

"I don't know. I don't think there's anyone up there." She sounded very despondent.

"Well, I know someone is up there," I told her, "and I know that he answers prayers. He's answered mine. He'll answer yours."

We talked for quite a while about things she could do in her quest for a testimony. She still hadn't forgiven herself—she needed to work on that. We also talked about church attendance, scripture study, wholesome activities, and associating with others who lived righteously and set good examples for her.

Before we hung up, Brooke promised that she'd continue praying.

I kept Brooke in my prayers, as well. I'd had a dark time in my life when I'd thought no one cared or heard my pleas, so I had empathy for what she was feeling. But I also knew that the temporary darkness eventually yielded to light; and in retrospect, I could see clearly that many of my prayers had indeed been answered during that period. It had taken the perspective of time to teach me that important lesson.

A month later, during my nightly prayer, I mentioned Brooke's name and felt an urgent need to write her a letter. I promised to write the next afternoon, and proceeded to pray, but I found that I could not get beyond thoughts of Brooke, and the idea that I must write to her continued to press itself into my mind.

I flipped on the light and jotted a quick reminder on the pad of paper I keep close to my bed: "Write to Brooke!" Then I turned off the light and tried to go to sleep.

But sleep eluded me. After silently singing a few songs that usually put me to sleep within minutes, I gave up the idea of sleep. I turned on the light again and reached for a book, intending to read for a while, but there was that note about Brooke, and I felt pushed to act on it.

I climbed out of bed, stepped into my slippers, and went downstairs to my kitchen table. I wrote a letter to Brooke, explaining that she was on my mind. I expressed my love and concern for her and then wrote more about prayer, answers, and testimony.

When I finished the letter, I addressed and stamped it and then set it on the counter to mail the next morning. I turned off the kitchen light and began climbing the stairs to my bedroom when I was struck with the urgent thought that I should mail the letter that night. That seemed ridiculous to me, but I was beyond argument, so I turned around, grabbed the letter and my purse, and got into my car. I drove to the nearest post office box, the one I knew had the earliest morning pick-up, dropped the letter into it, and then drove home.

This time, when I climbed in bed, I dropped off to sleep instantly.

I forgot about the letter in the week's flurry of activities. I remembered, however, to pray for Brooke.

On Saturday, I was pleased to see a letter from her in my mailbox. She wrote to tell me that my letter to her was dated on "the worst day of my life! Your letter was well-received. That night I sat in front of the temple until about 3:00 A.M. I don't know what I was doing: I just sat there and cried."

Later in the letter she wrote, "I have prayed every night since I have been here. I feel so unheard! I'm not asking for any answers right now, but I at least want to feel like God is there, listening. It is so hard to kneel down thinking, 'What's the use? No one is listening.' "

I disagreed with Brooke. I knew someone was listening. I knew it was no coincidence that I had written her a letter on the "worst day" of her life. I had been prompted to act to meet a need I could not have known nor anticipated on my own: I had been moved out of bed and had felt the necessity to write that letter before I went to sleep. It had proved to be important that my letter exhibit that specific date. When I wrote the letter, I hadn't known what Brooke needed, so I'd simply written what came to mind.

Now, I knew: that letter provided Brooke with physical evidence that her prayers were being heard, though she didn't realize that yet. On the "worst day" of Brooke's life, the Spirit had alerted me that she had an acute need to hear from me, one that could not wait until the next day, and, after some resistance on my part, I had finally been prodded to act.

I went straight to the phone and called Brooke. I told her the circumstances of my writing that letter. During the conversation, I emphasized a point about prayer that I knew to be true: God often answers our prayers or sends help, comfort, aid, and assistance through other people.

Brooke responded, "I see what you mean."

Much time has passed since that conversation about prayer. As Brooke persisted in daily prayer and continued to nurture a fledgling testimony, she discovered the many ways God answers prayers. She gained a testimony that someone was there when she prayed: Heavenly Father was always listening.

I have felt great joy watching Brooke grow and progress in the gospel. Today, she is a mature young woman whose happiness is not an act. If she says she's fine, she means it. Best of all, she knows that God not only listens to her but loves her.

Because Brooke has resolved many of her problems, she has moved beyond her own concerns to the needs of others. She conscientiously seeks to serve: she has often taken action to help, assist, lift, and teach those around her.

In fact, Brooke is now serving a mission. When I asked her where she wanted to go, she answered, "Somewhere challenging. I've prayed that I be sent to a 'hard' mission."

She got what she prayed for.

Feed My Sheep

Lovest thou me? And [Peter] said unto him, Lord, thou knowest all things; thou knowest that I love thee. Jesus saith unto him, Feed my sheep.
— John 21:17

The final chapter of John tells the story of Christ's appearance to the disciples after his crucifixion. "Lovest thou me?" he asks Peter, three different times. And when Peter repeatedly declares his love, Christ challenges him with the statement, "Feed my lambs," and then, "Feed my sheep," and, a third time, "Feed my sheep."

As I have taught teenagers, I have come to understand that though there is much to be learned through a broad interpretation of these words, there is also value in taking the Lord's words literally. I have a strong testimony of the potent power of simply feeding (as in doughnuts, pizza, ice cream, pancakes, etc.) teenage "sheep."

Gary was the first person who taught me that great but simple lesson. When I was teaching early-morning seminary, I usually brought doughnuts each Friday to celebrate that we had all survived another week of intense study and limited sleep. As is the case with many early-morning seminary teachers, most of my modest salary was quickly reinvested in the students in the form of food. This group favored doughnuts, so I listed each student's favorite kind beside his or her name and birth date on my roll. On Fridays, before going to the real-estate office where we held our seminary class, I'd stop at the doughnut shop to pick up wonderfully fresh, hot pastries in the flavors and variety listed on my roll.

I'd repeat the ritual randomly on other days throughout the month. It was my way of keeping my students guessing when doughnuts would appear stacked in two red and white boxes on top of the heavy load of scriptures and binders I hauled into the office from the trunk of my car each day.

One predawn morning, Gary walked into class, ten minutes late. He looked scruffy and half-asleep. He'd forgotten to comb his hair. As he passed by me on the way to his chair, he apologized for his tardiness, explaining that he'd been up late the night before studying for a test and had set his alarm for the last possible minute, wanting to claim each extra second of precious sleep. He'd underestimated the time he needed to get to the building, however. Then he said, "When my alarm went off this morning, I wanted to turn it off and go back to sleep. I figured Mom wouldn't mind if I missed seminary this morning. But just as I was rolling over I thought, 'Maybe Sister Bowen will have doughnuts this morning.' I thought about a nice, warm doughnut waiting for me in the box and knew that Brian would beg you for it if I didn't show up, so I got up, threw on my clothes, and came."

Then, Gary looked at my stack of books and grinned when he saw the familiar red and white box from the doughnut shop. "See!" he declared, "The Spirit never lies. I was prompted to come, and there's my immediate blessing."

The class laughed as Gary claimed his doughnut and bit into it with a final greeting directed at Brian, "Eat your heart out!"

The power of the warm doughnut rarely failed me. Teenagers

are motivated in seemingly irrational ways by food. I soon started a related motivational program with my seminary students: positive behavior earned Bowen Bucks — paper money that I could hand to them to reinforce good deeds or behavior. A student who accumulated enough Bowen Bucks could redeem them for a meal at my house, or a group trip to a local pizza restaurant, or a box of — you guessed it — doughnuts. I was amazed by what these kids would do to earn the right to come to my house to eat or go out for pizza: they did extra service projects, read extra chapters in their scriptures, cleaned up the real-estate office, helped me with class projects, competed vigorously in scripture chases or scripture basketball, and stopped missing classes.

The night before the first payoff, a fondue party at my home, I explained to my husband how the system worked and recounted the good work of my students. Every one of them had earned the right to come to the party. The cumulative tally was impressive.

"They did all this just to stick bread chunks in some melted cheese?" Scott asked.

"They were probably more motivated by the prospect of dipping fresh fruit in the dessert chocolate."

"Well, if that's all it takes to get them to do all these good things, let's keep feeding them," he declared.

And since that moment, we have. We've taken kids out for pizza and every variety of ethnic food; we've gathered students in our home for brunches, lunches, dinners, and desserts; we've baked enough cakes, brownies, and cookies to keep Betty Crocker in business, as we've celebrated individual birthdays and other special events; and we've served homemade pie and ice cream after general Church broadcasts for more than fifteen years.

At the beginning of each seminary year, the students fill out a questionnaire. One question is, "What do you need from me and this class?" Without exception, every year I get a statement like "Quality food."

Not long ago, my Sunday School class came for waffles on an out-of-school Friday (yes, they could also bring friends). Fifteen minutes before they were to gather, Nick's mother called me.

"Nick tells me you're feeding these kids again."

I laughed. "He's right. It's very informal, though. They'll have to cook most of it themselves. Is there a problem?"

"No," she said, "I just can't figure out why you're willing to do it. Don't get me wrong, he's so excited that he's downstairs ironing his own shirt, which is pretty unbelievable. And he cleaned his room this morning to earn the privilege of leaving the house. I just wanted to make sure he was really invited."

I assured her that he was and hung up, smiling. Why do I do this? Nick's mom isn't the first to ask the question. My answer comes quickly: because I believe in "other" classrooms — those not in meetinghouses.

You see, while teenagers are eating, they also talk, tease, and tell stories; and in the process, they drop a truckload of valuable information each and every time they gather. That information helps me know what lessons to prepare, who is lonely, who is being left out, who is having trouble at home, and who needs to be steered gently to the bishop. And I have never, not even once, had a group of kids gather for either a little treat or a full meal when one of them (at least one, and sometimes five or six) hasn't hung around to talk after the other kids have left. Any teacher knows that the most valuable teaching is done one-to-one. Those are the moments when a teacher can have the greatest influence.

There are other reasons I feed teenage sheep: to reward positive behavior, to motivate them to do good works, to get them together socially in a situation where they can't leave anyone out, and to teach them to feel comfortable around me. When they feel comfortable with me, then they know they can come to me when they need help.

"Feed my sheep." It is a simple admonition. It is a small thing, really, to bake brownies, to cook pancakes, to sit and visit in my living room for an hour. By heeding this simple statement literally, I have found the door opened for me to witness miracles. "And out of small things proceedeth that which is great" (D&C 64:33).

I keep feeding teenagers.

Potential and Power

For the power is in them, wherein they are agents unto themselves.

— Doctrine & Covenants 58:28

Amy was a bright student, a talented athlete, and a gentle soul. She was also part of a family that wrestled with the tough issues of alcoholism, multiple divorces, and abuse. Though Amy actively participated in the ward, her stepfather was not a member of the Church, and her mother was only partially active.

Adept at hiding the pain and even the existence of her family trials, Amy never gave anyone a clue that things were tough at home. I knew better, however, because I was her mother's visiting teacher and friend.

I worried about Amy. I could see her potential but feared that she was scarred and scared by her family's dysfunction. What would her future be after high school? Would she repeat the damaging family cycles or would she somehow rise above them, blessing generations with her decisions and actions? Oh, how I wanted her to break away from those cycles and soar!

The oldest of several children, Amy was often needed at home to help care for the younger ones. I watched her pass up opportunities for her own growth and development to accommodate family demands. There was no money for college, though Amy definitely had the ability to handle a tough academic course.

At home one night, I confided in my husband. He knew of Amy's family's difficulties, so no confidences were broken.

"I've been watching Amy," I told him. "She's very bright, you know. I'm sure she has the grades to get into BYU, but I'm afraid she'll never have the chance to go there."

Playing devil's advocate, my husband said, "That doesn't mean she can't go to college. The local community college is not expensive, so she can still get an education."

"I know. She can live at home and take classes, but even then, she'll have to work to support herself. It will take her years to finish at a snail's pace. Am I wrong to want more than that for her? She has a strong testimony, and she needs a spiritually nourishing environment. You know she doesn't get that at home."

"So, what do you want to do?"

"I wish there were a way we could help her get to BYU. Can't you see what that experience would do for her? I'd be happy if she could go just for a year, if she could just get a chance to break out and see what life could hold for her. I think about it every time I'm with her. She has so much potential. So much promise."

"What does Amy have to say about her future plans?" my husband asked.

"I've asked her, and she says she'll apply to BYU and work two after-school jobs. If she can save enough money, and if she gets accepted, maybe she'll be able to go to Provo for one year. Those are big if's."

Scott thought for a minute then said, "Well, we can hire her to work for us when we need a sitter or odd jobs done. And maybe, if she makes it to the Y, we can send an occasional check to help her out with expenses. But, honey, you keep talking about how bright and wonderful Amy is. Don't make the mistake of underestimating her ability to solve problems."

As it turned out, I was guilty of underestimating the abilities, insight, determination, and power of just about everyone involved in Amy's life.

First of all, Amy's mother, Nancy, surprised me. She told me, "I really struggle with the idea that Amy will be gone next year, but I want her to have the chance to make something good of her life, so I'm going to do everything I can to help her get to BYU."

"But I thought you needed her to stay home, so she could help you with the other children."

"I do, but she needs to go more than I need her to stay." Nancy confided that she had started working with a family therapist who was helping her to deal with her own emotional wounds: she was determined to emerge a healthy person and wanted her children to join her in family therapy, so that they could mend and grow also. That was an important first step.

The second person to surprise me was Amy. I followed my husband's suggestion and hired her to help with the children and do odd jobs around the house. That gave me the chance to get past the cheerful facade Amy wore to protect the real Amy. She began to confide some of her hopes and fears about her future. I was startled (and delighted!) by the determination in her voice when she spoke of her goals.

"Sister Bowen, I don't know how I'm going to do it, but I'm going to BYU. I'm sure I'll be accepted, and I'm going to work every minute until then to pull the money together to go. Nothing's going to stop me."

And nothing did. The acceptance came through. True to her word, Amy worked two jobs after school and on Saturdays until she graduated, and then she worked every minute she could through the summer. When September came, she had money for tuition, books, and housing. She'd get a job to help finance monthly living expenses.

Amy thrived at the Y. I loved reading her letters, witnessing how her testimony grew, and how she quickly broadened the circle of her experience. She loved attending devotionals. She devoured her course work and earned excellent grades. She enjoyed her roommates and the other students in her college ward. And she dated a lot, a new dimension in her social life, because she'd rarely dated in high school.

She worked with a family therapist, too, continuing on the path her mother had blazed. Slowly Amy began healing the deep family wounds that could have paralyzed her, had she and Nancy not been so determined to grow beyond them.

By spring, she faced the bleak realities of running out of money. Amy had worked as hard as she could as a waitress at a restaurant, but even then she could manage to earn only living expenses. She had no way of raising tuition money for the next year, and scholarship money was scarce, so she knew she'd have to return home to work until she had enough money to return to Provo. Whenever that would be.

Oh, how I wished I could just give her the tuition money. I wished I could hire her to work for me at a generous wage; however, I was helpless to do anything but cheer Amy on.

When September rolled around, and the other college students in the ward left for Ricks or BYU, Amy was left behind. She remained cheerful and determined. She was working two jobs. She bought an old car, because she had to provide her own transportation to her jobs and to the community college, where she enrolled in a couple of classes to keep on track.

I worried. I'd seen the scenario too many times: kids returned home from college and never went back again. Also, Nancy confided in me that things were not great at home: as the family members struggled to deal with their past and their emerging senses of self, a lot of friction developed. Nancy often wondered if she'd made a mistake to try to change: the process was so painful.

I often checked on Amy to see how she was doing.

"I'm okay," she'd say, shrugging. "I'll tell you something, Sister Bowen. I can't wait to get back up to Provo. I miss it terribly. I'm not going to let myself get stuck in this yucky routine. You just watch—I'm going back there."

I watched. In January, Amy returned to Provo, along with the other kids returning from Christmas vacation: after working hard for nine months, she had accumulated just enough money for rent, tuition, and books. She'd find a job to pay for the necessity of eating.

During that semester, Amy discovered her major. She took a psychology class and loved every second of it. Combined with her own experience and growth through family therapy, Amy set a goal for herself: she would become a therapist.

When Amy returned home in April, she told me she wasn't going to sit out of college any more. She would work as hard as she could all summer, but she was going back to BYU in the fall. She had fasted and prayed about it, and she felt that that was the best decision she could make. If she had enough money, she'd enroll in classes. If she didn't, then she'd either work full-time in Provo or take out student loans. She'd figure it out when she got there.

I asked about her classes and her grades: she'd absolutely thrived in the college environment, and she'd made the dean's list to prove it.

That summer, my family and I moved away. Before moving,

I asked her to keep me posted about how things worked out for her in the fall, and she promised she would.

We were all in for a big surprise when Amy returned to Provo the next time. Though it's been years since this happened, the story still makes me smile.

Amy had fasted and prayed about her decision to return to Provo in the fall. She felt calm about the decision, even though she lacked the money to enroll for the semester. She had enough money to pay either room and board, or tuition, but not both. Still, following her heart and the whisperings of the Spirit, Amy packed up her old car and took off for Provo at the end of August.

When she went to campus to inquire about financial aid, the registrar informed her that her tuition had already been paid. Amy was shocked. Sure that there had been a mistake, she asked the registrar to check the information again.

No, there was no mistake. Amy's tuition for the semester had been paid in full. She could complete her registration on the spot.

Amy was stunned. Who could have paid her tuition? Her mind raced through the names of people she knew were capable of assisting her like that but couldn't pinpoint anyone who would really do this. Yet, someone had. Who? It was an exciting mystery.

While she finished registering, Amy uttered prayer after grateful prayer for the anonymous person or people who had perceived her need and answered with such generosity.

Still in utter amazement, Amy returned to her apartment. There, she had another shock: when she went to the office to pay her rent, the manager told her that her rent had been paid for the entire semester. By this time, Amy was almost apoplectic. She grabbed the phone and called home, wondering if her parents knew anything about these payments.

Her parents were as shocked as Amy was. They knew nothing

about these generous acts. They, too, were delighted — and grateful. They suggested that Amy call the bishop.

The bishop was the only one who was not surprised. Yes, he knew about these kind acts. Yes, he knew who Amy's benefactors were. No, he would not tell her anything about them, but this: they were ward members who had watched Amy struggle to complete her college education at BYU, and they wanted to assist her towards that worthy goal. Her part of the bargain was to earn her own living expenses and to work as hard she could in her classes.

When Amy shared the story with me, I wept. There are some mighty amazing people on the face of the earth! And some of them lived in our old ward. My husband and I had desired to assist Amy financially but had been unable. Yet, here were people who had the wherewithal to help — and they had. Amy's life was changed by their sensitivity and kindness.

Amy later shared an additional bonus with me, after she'd gone home for Christmas vacation that year. "I sat in church that Christmas Sunday and studied the faces of the people in the rows," Amy said. "I looked at every face and asked myself, 'Is he or she the one?' You know what, Annette? There were dozens of people there who could have been my generous friends. Why, any of these people could have helped me! It changed the way I looked at them. It made me love every one of them more than ever. It also changed the way I looked at myself. Somewhere in the chapel, individuals were sitting who believed in me and my potential. Someone singing the same hymn that I was singing had also paid for my classes and put a roof over my head. I could not express my gratitude to them individually, but I could express my thanks to Heavenly Father and hope that he would let them know how thankful I was for their kindness."

I followed Amy's college career for the next few years. I don't know how often her tuition and rent were paid for her, but I know that Amy never had to drop out of BYU again. She continued to work for her living expenses, and she continued to study hard in her classes. She was motivated by the knowledge that back home there were many people who believed in her.

Amy graduated from BYU with honors, election to several honor societies, and a degree in psychology. By then, she under-stood her own potential and her own power. By then, I had learned not to underestimate her abilities: I was no longer surprised by her determination nor by her achievements. I was simply and intensely proud of her. I knew that Amy could do anything she decided to do. She knew she had the power to determine the course of her life, and she knew, from experience, that she would receive assistance from the Lord and from those around her when she needed it.

That fall I received a long letter from Amy. She was planning to be married to a fine returned missionary in the Mesa Temple in October. Her mother and father would be in Mesa for the wedding but would not be able to enter the temple. Would I stand in for her mother?

I was moved by her request but had a scheduling conflict. I discussed the problem with my husband, and then we took the problem to the Lord. After fasting and praying, I felt certain that I should be in Arizona with Amy that weekend. The next problem was that I didn't have the money for my transportation.

My husband told me to book a plane ticket for the wedding and to tell Amy that I would be with her when she was married. He felt impressed to tell me that the money for the fare would not be a problem. We talked again about the miracles we'd wit-nessed in Amy's life and decided to follow these promptings with faith. We'd need a miracle of our own to make my journey possible.

It was a hot October morning when I entered the Mesa

Temple to find Amy waiting for me. She was gorgeous beyond description. I thought of her as I first knew her: a quiet, struggling young teenager wearing a brave face to hide her troubles. Now, standing before me in this lovely brides' room in the Lord's temple was a self-assured, intelligent, magnificently beautiful woman.

As I helped her slip into her wedding gown, I asked her how she felt.

"I'm scared to death," she said honestly. "Because of all the studying I've done, I know what problems I could face in a marriage."

"You've also learned about communication and coping with problems. You're very well equipped to handle the challenges that marriage will bring," I assured her.

"But everything I know is theory—here comes the practical application."

"You'll be fine!" I whispered as I hugged her.

"I hope so," she sighed. "Well, here goes . . . " she said, and we left the brides' room.

The sealing room was filled with the Spirit. How grateful I was to be there. How glad I was that my husband had encouraged me to take this trip.

I admired the two young people who knelt at the altar. Individually they had overcome terrific obstacles to be who and where they were: they would love and cherish each other and support and nurture each other. Theirs was a marriage of much potential and promise.

Outside the temple, I felt my heart split with sadness when I saw Nancy waiting outside the door. If only she could have been at Amy's side for this important occasion.

Nancy was cheerful and magnanimous. As she hugged me in greeting, she said, "I decided that if I couldn't be with Amy this morning, you were the one person I'd choose to take my place.

Thank you for coming. I needed you to do this for me." As we walked down the temple stairs together, she took hold of my hand, saying, "Haven't you watched us all come a long way over the years?"

Yes, I had. And I had been richly blessed and inspired, witnessing their journey.

After I returned home from that wonderful weekend, I opened my mail to discover a check for the exact amount of my plane fare. A friend of mine had sent it to liquidate a long-standing debt — one I had forgotten.

Whenever I think of Amy, I am reminded that God not only guides our journeys but provides for them as well, if we'll but trust in his loving hand. He has given each of us potential and power and promise. "Whereby are given unto us exceeding great and precious promises: that by these ye might be partakers of the divine nature" (2 Peter 1:4).

He invites all of us to partake.

Neighbors

*And now, if your joy will be great with one soul that you
have brought unto me into the kingdom of my Father,
how great will be your joy if you should bring many souls
unto me!*
— *Doctrine & Covenants 18:16*

Sarah and Ted lived across the street from each other. They
were the same age; they'd attended school together from grade
school on; and they'd played together in the neighborhood. By
the time they reached high school, they were good friends.

They could talk to each other. When they began to notice
members of the opposite sex, they could confide in each other.
That neighborly counsel was very helpful: Ted could interpret
boys' actions for Sarah, and Sarah could tell Ted what the girls
were saying about him. They were a great pair of buddies.

They supported one another. Sarah was happy when Ted tried
out for the wrestling team and made it. She encouraged Ted to
keep to his weight-training program and believed in his athletic
abilities. Ted supported Sarah's decision to try out for the gym-
nastics team. He cheered for her when she competed and occasionally critiqued routines when she practiced them at home.

They helped each other to learn new things: Sarah taught

97

Ted how to do flips on her family's trampoline, and Ted helped Sarah with the occasional difficult homework assignment.

Ted and Sarah were each blessed with loving, supportive, and devoted parents.

Sarah was a Mormon. She was one of seven children and lived in a household that at times nearly rocked on its foundation. Ted's family had no religious affiliations. He had just one brother, and he was away at college. Ted's house was always quiet.

When Ted was a sophomore, he started paying more attention to things going on at Sarah's house. He knew he was always welcome in her home, and he enjoyed being included in some of the family's activities. He noticed that there was "something different" about the way he felt when he was in Sarah's home.

Sarah, by that time, was eager to teach Ted something other than trampoline routines: she wanted to teach him about the gospel. She couldn't think of anything more valuable that she could share with a friend.

Sarah had already brought one friend into the Church. That experience gave her confidence to talk about the Church with her friends whereas other Mormon kids her age usually avoided the topic.

After prayerful consideration, Sarah decided it was time to talk to Ted about her own religious beliefs. She prayed daily that she would be guided to say and do the right thing. She promised to set a good example for Ted and asked the Lord to help her with her missionary efforts. She knew that she could receive divine assistance in teaching Ted about the gospel.

She told her family about her goal. She asked for their assistance in teaching Ted and "loving" him into the Church. They all loved Ted, anyway, and they felt that he might be ready to be taught the gospel.

Sarah's mother and I were friends, and we talked often. During one of our visits, she told me about Sarah's goal to encourage Ted to receive "the lessons" from the missionaries.

I was interested in the process, because I hesitated to talk about the Church with others. I was impressed by Sarah's boldness and her desire to be a missionary.

I had not yet met Ted. I guessed who he was, however, because I'd often seen her in the company of a handsome, blond young man, talking on her lawn, or jumping on the trampoline, or sitting together on a stump on the street's "island."

Sarah's mom kept me posted about Sarah's missionary progress. "She's told him about the preexistence," I was told. "She's talked to him about baptism and what it symbolizes," I heard next. "She's told him all about the Church youth programs. And something must be touching him, because Ted's been seeking out other Mormon kids at school and asking them about the Church."

Next, I heard about a special family home evening planned just for Ted. Sarah's parents prepared a lesson on the plan of salvation. Ted listened and then asked many questions. The Spirit was present in the home, and everyone felt it.

During the following week, a student of mine asked me some interesting doctrinal questions. "I've got to have these answers backed up with scripture references," he explained, "because there's this really cool guy at school who's drilling me about the Church."

"Is his name Ted?" I asked.

"How did you know?" he wondered.

"I've been hearing about him and Sarah," I replied. "Tell me what you know about him."

"Well, he's a super good student. Straight A's. That kind of guy. He's a wrestler. He's got high standards. In fact, he told me that he's been drawn to me because he knows I don't drink or mess around with girls and that kind of stuff. I guess the best way I can describe him is that he's a 'dry Mormon.' "

I reported the conversation to Sarah's mom. She was elated. "And, I've got some news for you. I did something rather bold today. I looked across the street at Ted's house and thought about his parents. They've got to be wondering about all this discussion about the Church; so, I decided to wrap up a Book of Mormon, take it over there, and give them an explanation about the Church and our beliefs. Can you believe I did that?"

"Good for you!" I said. "How did it go?"

"Great! Ted's mother was home. I told her that we'd really grown to love Ted over the years and that he and Sarah were having a lot of conversations about our church. I explained that we didn't want to overstep our bounds, so I wanted to make sure that was all okay with her. Then I gave her a copy of the Book of Mormon, told her what it was, and suggested that she might want to read it. Then I told her I'd be available to answer any questions she might have about our church as a result of Ted's inquiries. She was very gracious about the whole thing. It turns out that she has some distant relatives who are Mormons. She said that she was aware of Ted's interest in the Church and that she and her husband trusted Ted to make wise decisions. She told me that they had always supported Ted in everything he'd undertaken and were ready to let whatever happened, happen."

"Well, she's certainly open-minded, isn't she?" I said.

"I walked away from her door with great respect for her. I don't think I would be so gracious, if the tables were turned."

"Good point," I said. "This whole process could be a little frightening for a parent, couldn't it?"

"Yes, and I really think they're wonderful to allow Ted to pursue this interest in the Church. Well," she sighed, "I guess we'll just wait to see what happens next!"

What happened next was that Ted started reading the Book of Mormon. He had dozens of questions, but he admitted that he felt a special spirit when he read. Then he confided in Sarah that the other members of his family had been baptized at some point in their lives but he'd never been baptized, and that bothered him.

That was the opening Sarah was looking for. She invited Ted to meet with the missionaries, and he hesitantly agreed.

We had a new set of elders in our ward. One of them was from Chile. In a lifetime of Church membership, I'd never known a missionary from a foreign country to serve in my area. Neither had most of the other members of my ward. We were in for a treat, for this humble young man brought an incredibly sweet spirit with him.

He came to us straight out of the Missionary Training Center. Struggling with a new language, he stood to bear his testimony on his first Sunday with us. He explained that he didn't have a large English vocabulary, so, instead of speaking to us, he wished to sing his testimony. In Spanish, he sang the beautiful words of a song familiar to many of us, "Whom Shall I Serve?" By the time he was finished, there was not a dry eye in the chapel.

If ever there was a missionary prepared to touch Ted and to reach him, this elder was the one.

The next week, Ted began taking the lessons. These missionary meetings took place in Sarah's home. Ted's parents supported Ted's interest in the Church, but they declined to participate with him.

After each lesson, a new lesson time was scheduled.

Ted was very impressed by the messages the missionaries taught and by the Spirit that was present during their discussions. He knew these young men were only a few years older than he, but they seemed to know so much. And he was especially drawn to the Chilean elder.

Sarah was thrilled about Ted's progress. She continued to pray for guidance, and she prayed for Ted to feel the Spirit and to gain a testimony.

Within the month, Ted had set a date for his baptism.

At the baptismal service, I kept my eye on Sarah. In a few short months, she would be a student in my class. Little did she know that she had already taught me quite a bit by her fine example as a missionary.

Sarah's joy could not be contained. The light within her radiated and beamed—I'd dare say she glowed! She had introduced her friend to the gospel, and he had listened and responded. After Ted's baptism and confirmation, Sarah told us that it was the happiest moment of her life.

Because Ted was sixteen at the time of his baptism, he ended up in my Sunday School class. Ted was a bright, articulate young man. His eyes sparkled. He had a keen mind. He was a natural leader. Ted proved to be one of those kids who stands out in any crowd. But that's another story. (See "Reaching for the Stars.")

As far as this story goes, there are still two short anecdotes to tell.

The first: When Ted was baptized, Sarah was awaiting her sixteenth birthday. When Sarah's landmark birthday finally rolled around, Ted invited her out for her first date. After all, isn't that what good neighbors are for?

The second: Sarah is now a student at Ricks College. She struggled with the decision of where to attend school. She had made plans other than attending Ricks, but she and her parents received strong promptings that Sarah needed to be in Rexburg. She followed those promptings of the Spirit.

When she made her first visit home from college, I was anxious to talk with her. I gave her a big welcome-home hug and asked her about her experience in Rexburg.

"Oh, Sister Bowen, it's been good and it's been bad," she told me. "I really miss my family. School's okay. I miss Ted. But, I guess all that's normal. The thing that really bothered me about going to Ricks was that I thought there are only Mormons in Rexburg. I wanted to do more missionary work, and I couldn't figure out how I was going to do that at Ricks."

Then she flashed a mischievous smile. "But I've found out something: half the members of the football team are not members of the Church."

I could tell there was more to the story, so I encouraged her to continue. "And?"

"And, I'm friends with a Catholic guy right now. He's already taken the discussions once, but I think I can get him to take them again." Sarah's eyes sparkled with hope and joy and a new missionary challenge.

Turn on the water in the font.

Reaching for the Stars

Then, my brethren, ye shall reap the rewards of your faith,
and your diligence, and patience, and long-suffering.
— Alma 32:43

Ted is a remarkable young man who began his quest to find "the right church" when he was sixteen years old.

A member of the wrestling team at Newport High School for four years, Ted won the conference title in his weight division during his junior year; as a senior, Ted took sixth in the state in his weight division. Ted also played football for four years. During his senior year, his team reached the state AAA quarter-finals. When he graduated from high school, Ted was recognized as an Army Reserve National Scholar Athlete.

Yes, Ted is also a scholar: a 4.0 student in high school, Ted was accepted at many of the country's most prestigious universities. A National Merit Commended Scholar, Ted earned a Washington State honors award, a Washington Principals' Scholars Award, and four local awards, including a scholarship awarded to the most outstanding male graduate.

Ted is also a leader. He served as president of the junior class at his high school and as student body vice president. In his ward, Ted served as first assistant to his bishop in leading the priests quorum.

Ted has other talents as well. He played the trumpet in a band for seven years. And he wrote for his high school paper and served on the staff.

Does Ted sound too good to be true? Well, I've had the privilege of working with him, and he's for real. He's simply a nice guy. You'd think he'd be conceited, but he's not. Blessed with an abundance of talent and intellect, Ted is a hard worker who has developed the self-discipline necessary to be a highly successful young man. I have profited from his fine example, as have many others around him. I'm grateful that Ted went searching for truth and found it in the gospel.

I asked Ted to tell me the story of his conversion.

"I had never been baptized into any church, even though the other members of my family had been baptized as infants. When I was around ten or twelve, it bothered me that I hadn't been baptized. I thought that it was important, and I wondered about it."

The thought continued to nag at Ted, and he concluded that getting baptized was "probably something I needed to do." When he was in high school, Ted wanted involvement in a church, but he didn't know which one. He said, "I prayed a couple of nights that Heavenly Father would lead me to the right church." He told no one about his yearnings.

At the time, Ted lived across the street from the Larsens, who are dedicated Latter-day Saints. Ted had been good friends with Sarah for years, since they were children. "Within a couple of weeks from the time I'd prayed about a church, Sarah asked me if I wanted to go to church with her." Ted was surprised, because she didn't know of his quest, but he agreed to attend church with her the following Sunday.

Ted had a journalism class with Bill, another LDS student at Newport High School. "Bill was a lot of fun, and somehow I knew he was Mormon. During that week I asked him questions about the Church while we were in class."

Ted attended church with the Larsens the following Sunday. He liked everything he saw. Afterwards, Sarah asked, "Would you like to talk to the missionaries?" Ted said yes, though he wasn't sure what missionaries were.

Ted met Elder Nyman, from Arizona, and Elder Martinez, from Chile, in the Larsens' home. Three weeks into the discussions, the Larsens took Ted on a quick trip to Utah. Ted relates, "I was wondering about what I was learning, and visiting Temple Square was a big deal for me."

Ted continued the missionary discussions when he returned home. "In every discussion I'd hear something that made me think, 'I've heard this before,' or 'I totally believe that!'" He agreed with the baptism age, "because it allows individuals to choose for themselves." He especially liked what he learned about the three degrees of glory. "I'd always thought there can't be just heaven and hell. I thought there should be a distinction between someone who always tried to do what's right and someone who's a basically good person but who didn't bother keeping the commandments. So, the idea of kingdoms sounded right to me. I like the promise that we can return to the celestial kingdom—the whole plan of salvation."

"Everything matched perfectly, and it went on like that," Ted told me about his continued meetings with the missionaries. "Before I even finished the Book of Mormon, I thought, 'This is the true church.' I didn't even finish the Book of Mormon until after I was baptized."

I wondered how his parents had responded to the missionary discussions and Ted's decision to be baptized.

"My parents were surprised when I set a baptism date, though they knew I had been meeting with the missionaries. They've given me every opportunity to do what I wanted to do, and they've always let me choose."

The Eatons continued to support their son in his choices, and they permitted him to be baptized. It helped that they felt good about other Mormons they knew. "My parents had a good image of Mormons. . . . We'd visited the Seattle Temple before it was dedicated, but I hadn't connected that with the Church at the time."

"I remember my dad telling me a long time ago about an experience when we lived in Michigan. He'd gone fishing with a friend who was a Church member. He'd had the greatest time. Dad told me he had the best impression of Mormons, because they never swore, and they didn't drink, and stuff like that."

So, Ted's parents felt that he was making a positive choice. "Their one reservation was they thought I'd face a lot of discrimination, being a Mormon, and I have already faced some."

I asked if that had been a problem for him. "No. I figure if something's true, you just make the sacrifice for it. That's not even an issue."

Ted was baptized by Brother Larsen, Sarah's father, six weeks after attending church for the first time. He knew his prayers had been answered: Heavenly Father had guided him to the right church.

Ted feels that Heavenly Father has continued to guide and direct him. Shortly after Ted was baptized, a new full-time elder was assigned to the area. Elder Preston had been attending the United States Naval Academy in Annapolis, Maryland, before leaving on his mission. He was a wrestler. He was a scholar. He and Ted were drawn to each other immediately.

Ted had always dreamed of going to Annapolis or West Point, and through his friendship with Elder Preston, he had the opportunity to learn about naval academy life as Elder Preston continued to teach Ted about the gospel.

Elder Preston was a role model for Ted. "Joe Preston has been a really great example and influence. I admire him. It seems that he has everything—he's a good wrestler, he's in good standing at the academy, and yet he made the sacrifice to take the time to go on a mission. I'm glad that he went on his mission, because he was an answer to a prayer for *me*."

When it came time for Ted to select a college, he faced some tough decisions: because of his outstanding record, he had many fine opportunities available to him. How could he make the right choice about his future? He made his decision a matter of prayer.

Ted applied to three top universities and to the three service academies. He applied for congressional appointments to the academies and was told that he ought to try for a vice-presidential appointment as well. The competition is tough for these prestigious appointments. Approximately six hundred applicants were applying for a handful of vice-presidential appointments.

Early one morning, Ted was awakened by a phone call from the White House. He was told that he needed to decide which academy he wanted to attend, because his name appeared on the list of top candidates from all three academies.

Ted had struggled through the process of making a decision. He had gathered information about the academies, and he had conferred with many people. Now he selected an academy and prayed for confirmation of his decision; however, he said, "It kept bugging me." So, Ted reconsidered his decision. "When I made the navy my number-one choice, I felt comfortable." Finally, he felt some peace: he would go to Annapolis. A prestigious nomination to the naval academy from the vice president of the United States followed this decision.

Ted is now at Annapolis. Joe Preston, his dear friend and role model, is a senior at the naval academy, and Ted is a plebe, or freshman.

Ted loves the challenges of academy life: "The naval academy offers a well-rounded experience—academics, athletics, discipline, with an emphasis on team effort. I like that environment. Whenever I get in an environment that really pushes me, I can thrive."

I asked him why he loved to be challenged and pushed so much.

"There's so much growth involved in challenges, in overcoming things," he said. "You learn so much that's not even related to what you're overcoming. There are a lot of life lessons to be learned through simple challenges."

Ted has plenty of challenges now, and because of the goals he has set for himself, he is guaranteed plenty of challenges in his future. Ted hopes to follow in Elder Preston's footsteps. Though he knows he'll have to resign his commission, and later apply to reenter the naval academy, he plans to serve a mission.

After his mission, he hopes to return to the naval academy to become a pilot of some sort of tactical aircraft. Ted hopes his training will lead to a career as an astronaut, for he is, literally, reaching for the stars. "I can't imagine anything being more fascinating than that," he said.

Ted also plans to marry in the temple and to rear a family in the Church. "And, eventually, maybe I'll go into politics." Ted smiled. "Maybe someday I'll even run for president of the United States."

"I like challenges," Ted told me. Then he smiled broadly. "I *love* challenges. I can accomplish anything I want to, as long as it's what the Lord wants me to do."

Ted has already proved to himself and others that he can usually reach the goals he sets for himself. Best of all, he knows he doesn't work alone. He appreciates the loving support of family and friends, and he is deeply grateful for the divine assistance he has had in his life. One of his favorite passages of scripture is "Search diligently, pray always, and be believing, and all things shall work together for your good, if ye walk uprightly and remember the covenant wherewith ye have covenanted one with another" (D&C 90:24).

Ted has set his sights on the stars. If Ted continues to work diligently, to pray always, and to obey the commandments, he will probably attain them, for he is an extraordinary young man.

The Least of These

Inasmuch as ye have done it unto one of the least of these my brethren, ye have done it unto me.
— Matthew 25:40

Philip was a troubled young man.

The other kids in the ward did not like him much. He irritated them. He had annoying habits like shaking his head when he talked and nervously rapping a pencil against his leg in class. He did not always attend to his personal hygiene. He said irrelevant things in classes and at activities, and he blurted out scripture passages whenever someone was doing something wrong. His nervous laugh drove some of my students up the wall.

Philip *was* hard to take in large doses. His habits *were* irritating. Often in class I'd have to stop and reexplain a point of the lesson, or I'd have to try to reel the discussion back in, after Philip grabbed a word or phrase and started to run with an unrelated story. Though I admired his knowledge of the scriptures, I understood why the other kids did not appreciate his impromptu mini sermons.

I figured that Philip was plunked down in my life to teach me patience, and I tried my best to be patient with him. To tolerate him. To keep him from disrupting the class too often.

Philip had been severely abused and neglected as a child, and the state had intervened to move Philip and his siblings into foster homes. He was emotionally handicapped: who wouldn't be, coming out of the nightmare that he called home?

His foster parents, members of our ward, were true saints to deal with him around the clock. They worked conscientiously to help him and direct his growth.

I didn't know what to do with Philip beyond being kind to him for an hour each Sunday and putting up with his distracting behaviors.

Philip soon taught me and many other members of our ward that he needed more than tolerance. Because of Philip, I learned that more was required of me than patience and token kindness. It was Philip who taught me what he needed. It was the Lord who taught me what was required of me to supply Philip with what he needed.

Philip struggled very hard against bad family patterns to change, to succeed, to be accepted, to be loved by others. He set goals for himself. He studied the scriptures every day. He got a job and rode his bike back and forth to work, up and down a steep hill, rain or shine. He attended school regularly and tried to do his homework. He never missed seminary, church, or a youth activity. Philip made every effort to be good. To be capable. To be lovable.

Regardless of his efforts, though, what Philip got back from me and many other members of the ward were patronizing smiles, occasional inquiries about how he was doing, and a lot of advice about what he should be doing.

That's not much for a young man simply seeking to feel a little love.

One weekend, Philip felt so desperate and frustrated that he ran away from his foster home. He took his scriptures and a backpack and headed into the hills behind their house. He wasn't sure if he'd come back or not. In fact, he wasn't sure if he wanted to live anymore.

He left a note saying so.

Philip's foster parents found the note. They'd been away from the house for several hours, so they didn't know how long Philip had been gone. Frightened, they sought advice.

Should they organize a search party, or should they wait to see if he'd come home? Since it was already late afternoon, and because of the tone of Philip's note, they decided not to wait for him to return. Instead, a group of searchers entered the woods to try to locate him before nightfall. To comb all the woods was an impossible task, because Philip had retreated into a huge forest preserve. After many hours, there was no trace of him, though one neighbor reported that he had seen Philip heading up a certain trail.

While the group searched, I waited at home. I was recovering from surgery at the time, so I could not join the search party. As the Saturday hours ticked slowly away, I found myself unable to immerse myself in any project. Nagging thoughts of Philip popped into my mind: I thought of times when he had probably been sending me a signal of need, and I hadn't answered; activities when he'd been left on the periphery, alone; moments of aggravation when he was vying for attention—any kind of attention.

That evening, as dusk deepened into dark, the worries mounted. Darkness fell, and the search party had to come in from the woods to wait for dawn to light their paths again.

Through the night, we sent frequent prayers heavenward. I arose twice to check the temperature, fearing a reading that would leave a young man frozen in the woods. Had Philip taken a jacket? I hoped he had.

As I stood on my balcony, shivering in the cold, I forced myself to face the possibility that Philip might not be alive. The elements would not kill him tonight, but what if he fell off a cliff, as another hiker recently had? What if he encountered a cougar or a bear? I knew there were many wild animals roaming the preserve. What if he took his own life? I could not tolerate that thought, so I fled from it.

I returned to the warmth of my family room, and sought solace in the scriptures. Needing the Savior's words, I began reading in Matthew. I read a few parables, and then I was stopped cold by Matthew 25. I had often read verses 35 through 40 and had loved them. They had frequently provided motivation for me to reach towards others: "And the King shall answer and say unto them, Verily I say unto you, Inasmuch as ye have done it unto one of the least of these my brethren, ye have done it unto me" (Matthew 25:40).

Surely, if there was a person within my reach who qualified as a "least of these, my brethren," Philip was one. I kept reading, measuring myself against this scriptural ruler. How had I treated Philip?

These next words hit hard.

"For I was an hungred, and ye gave me no meat: I was thirsty, and ye gave me no drink:

"I was a stranger, and ye took me not in: naked, and ye clothed me not: sick, and in prison, and ye visited me not.

"Then shall they also answer him, saying, Lord, when saw we thee an hungred, or athirst, or a stranger, or naked, or sick, or in prison, and did not minister unto thee?

"Then shall he answer them, saying, Verily I say unto you, Inasmuch as ye did it not to one of the least of these, ye did it not to me.

"And these shall go away into everlasting punishment: but the righteous into life eternal" (Matthew 25:42–46).

The Savior's words condemned my actions.

Philip hungered and thirsted for love and attention, and I had fed him crumbs of tolerance and drops of patience. Philip came to me a stranger, yearning to be accepted in a circle of friendship, and I had required him to change before I would let him in. Philip came to me naked, devoid of warm relationships, and I had withheld the cloak of fellowship. Philip came to me imprisoned by patterns of abuse and neglect, and I had not ministered adequately to him — failing to give him enough skills, strength, and encouragement to free himself.

On every count mentioned in the scripture, Philip had come to me; on every count, I had disappointed him. And, in failing to adequately serve Philip, I had failed to adequately serve the Lord.

I wept that night, begging for the Lord to preserve Philip's life, to protect him through the night, to bring him home. I needed another chance to learn to love him.

The next day was Sunday. At sunrise a new search party was formed, this one involving the other priests in Philip's quorum. They hunted all morning but could not find him.

At church the ward prayed for Philip's safety. We prayed that if he was lost, he would be found or that he would find the way home.

I felt the irony of that prayer. Philip was lost, in many ways. It was our duty as his brothers and sisters to find him and bring him home into a loving and supportive circle.

It was a sober group of teenagers that met with me during Sunday School. Knowing I could teach them no other lesson, I recounted what I had learned during the night. With broken hearts and contrite spirits, the group talked of ways they had failed Philip, and together we vowed to change.

I thought about how much Philip's presence was missed that day and realized that I would be profoundly grateful to have Philip there again in my classroom, interrupting my lesson, blurting out scripture verses, and rapping his pencil against his leg.

Philip came wandering back out of the woods later that Sunday. He was hungry, cold, shaken, and tired. He found food, warm clothing, comforting words of relief and joy, and a cozy bed awaiting him.

During his lonely hours in the woods, Philip had decided that he wanted to keep on living, to keep on trying. He'd prayed and read his beloved scriptures for what seemed like hours, and then he had started for home. Unfortunately, he became disoriented and could not find the right trail.

Trying not to panic and get himself in more trouble, he'd remembered a Scout lesson to "hug a tree." He stayed put, in hopes someone would find him. He had cried out for help, but no one had answered. He had not seen the search parties, but he thought he had heard them. He had waited through the long, dark night, clutching the scriptures he'd brought with him, for comfort. When he awoke, having finally dozed off in the wee hours, he waited through the morning to be found. Finally, fearing another night alone in the woods, and driven by hunger, he had prayed for guidance and was certain he had been led to the trail home.

When I saw Philip again, I threw my arms around him. I told him how frightened and concerned I had been when he was missing. Then I asked him what I could do to help him.

"Well, I could use another hug," Philip replied, shyly.

Such a simple request, easily granted. I hugged him again. I wondered how many hugs Philip had received in his lifetime.

I would guess that there had not been many, for every Sunday after that, after class was over, Philip would wait for a hug.

Before long, I could also add an "I love you" to the hug and mean it.

It turned out, after all, that a hug went a long way for Philip.

Philip's foster parents and other caring members of our ward doubled their efforts to help this young man. We stopped giving him "stones" and gave him the "bread" he needed (Matthew 7:9). He was counseled, encouraged, guided, and taught. The goals were simple: build Philip's self-esteem and teach him the skills he needed to become a self-reliant adult.

Philip graduated from high school and joined the army, something he'd always wanted to do. My family missed him, prayed for him, and wrote to him. Occasionally, we mailed off a box of goodies, knowing how much a surprise package would mean to him.

When he got out of the army, he lived in an apartment with some other young men and continued to successfully support himself. The last time we talked, he told me he was moving; but he did not give me a new phone number or address. Six months went by, and then late last night, after returning from a meeting, I heard his voice and this message on my telephone answering machine: "Hello! This is Philip. I really need to talk to you. Could you call me back, please? This is my new number. . . . "

He has been on my mind recently. Is it coincidence that he called yesterday?

I'll give him a call, and see what he needs. His requests are usually small, "I just wanted to hear your voice"; or, "I wanted to share some news with you"; or, "I'm having a hard time with something, and I thought it would help to talk it over with somebody." It costs me very little to be Philip's friend.

I will always be in Philip's debt, however, for what he taught me: a hug goes a long way, and for a love-starved person, the smallest act of kindness becomes enormous in significance. I am especially grateful for learning the lesson that I cannot fail the Philips in my life without failing the Lord.

Since Philip entered my life, I have kept looking for others like him. With eyes opened to see, tutored by the Lord, I have found many within easy reach.

The Path of Lies

I know that thou believest, but thou art possessed with a lying spirit, and ye have put off the Spirit of God that it may have no place in you.
— Alma 30:42

Carrie's lying started in high school. It was seemingly harmless then: just little things, like making excuses. "Nobody told me about the meeting," she'd tell her Laurel teacher, "so I didn't know about my assignment."

"I told you about the meeting and your assignment. In fact, I told you twice."

"Well, I didn't hear you," Carrie would retort.

The lies got more blatant. When a youth leader, hoping to help her, confronted her about rumors that she was partying, Carrie said, "Oh, I go to some of those parties, but I don't do what the other kids do." Problem was, other kids had seen her participating in unwholesome activities.

There were other rumors, too, and they were most worrisome. If they were true, Carrie was in big spiritual trouble. A concerned teacher went to the bishop, asking him to speak with Carrie.

The bishop had a long talk with Carrie, and he decided to continue meeting with her. He told her teacher, "I get the feeling that she's not telling me the whole truth. But I'll keep working with her. Maybe we can get to the heart of this."

At the end of the year, Carrie went off to Brigham Young University. Those of us who were concerned about her took that as a good sign: she had counseled with the bishop and cleared her interviews. We hoped and prayed that Carrie's rebellion and deceit had ended and that she would prosper in the spiritual environment at BYU.

During Christmas vacation, one of my former students came to see me. "I have a problem, Sister Bowen, and maybe you can help me decide what to do about it." He'd been invited to a party with a bunch of kids from our area who were attending school in Provo. At that party, he'd seen Carrie make choices that blatantly violated Church standards and invalidated her signature on her BYU standards contract. He wanted me to tell him what to do about it. He was sure she would know who had ratted, if he told anyone, and he wasn't comfortable with that.

I urged him to talk with her as a friend. I also asked him to consider telling the bishop so that he could help Carrie. I'm not sure if he did or not, but I'd guess that he didn't.

In April I attended some meetings in Provo. Wanting to see many of my former students while I was near campus, I organized a dinner and invited them to the party. Calls went out, spreading the invitation.

On the designated night, eighteen of my former students gathered. I was thrilled to see these friends again. Carrie did not show up, however, so I asked about her.

"I talked to her this afternoon, and she said she was coming," said one young woman who lived near Carrie.

A young man said, "Yeah, I ran into her on campus, and she said she'd see us all tonight."

"Well," I said, "when you see her, tell her that I missed her. And I was supposed to give her a hug from her mom."

After dinner, as we were leaving the restaurant, Melinda approached me. "Sister Bowen, do you have some time before you go back home? I really need to talk to you."

"Sure," I replied. "How about tomorrow afternoon? I'm free around two. Are you out of class by then?"

"Yes. Two would be great."

"Do you want to meet on campus, or would you like me to come to your apartment?"

She smiled. "Could you come to my apartment? That would be perfect. I need to tell you just one little thing tonight, though. It's about Carrie. You were wondering where she was tonight. I don't think she ever had any intention of coming. I don't think she dared see you."

I was startled by that statement. "Why?"

"Because she's afraid you'd pick up on something. You know how you've always taught us that the Holy Ghost helps you to discern."

A shock of worry surged through me. "Is there something wrong with Carrie?" I asked.

"Yes. That's one of the reasons I want to talk to you."

By that time, Melinda was being hailed across the parking lot by the kids who were giving her a ride back to her place. "Hey, I'd better run," she said.

"See you tomorrow, Melinda." My mind was already racing. What was wrong with Carrie?

The next afternoon, I talked with Melinda at her apartment. She had some challenges herself and wanted some friendly counsel. Eventually, the conversation swung around to Carrie.

"Carrie's in a lot of trouble," Melinda said. "She doesn't recognize it, but she's pretty scary."

"What kind of trouble?" I asked.

"Well, she's still partying. I don't think she ever stopped."

"Oh, come on, you know she cleaned up her act back home, or she wouldn't have cleared her bishop's interviews to come to BYU. Bishops conduct thorough interviews before signing those endorsement papers."

"She lied to him." Melinda shot at me, and it stung as it hit.

"How do you know?"

"Because she told me. She said that she didn't want to hurt him or her parents — they've always wanted her to come to BYU — so, she just lied to him."

I groaned. "So, the lying continues." I thought of other conversations I'd had with kids who had lied through interviews and their remorse about those lies. One kid had lied his way into the Missionary Training Center before his conscience stopped him and he went to the president of the MTC to confess. I had hoped Carrie had turned away from her lying.

Melinda interrupted my thoughts. "She's lying, big time. You're probably not going to be too thrilled to hear this, but I've got to tell you something else."

I braced myself for more bad news.

Melinda thought for a few seconds. "Carrie's on the Pill."

"Are you sure she's sexually active?" I asked Melinda.

"Sister Bowen, she told me herself, and I've seen the pills in her purse."

"What did you say?" I asked Melinda.

"I told her she was crazy. I told her she was headed for major trouble. She told me that she wouldn't get 'in trouble,' meaning pregnant, because she was on the Pill. So, I told her that wasn't what I meant. I told her that she'd lose the Holy Ghost and that she'd get kicked out of BYU, if someone reported her. You know what she said?"

I waited to hear.

"She said that nobody could prove anything. She told me that all you had to do if you got hauled in for a standards meeting or a bishop's interview was to lie."

I felt like someone had dropped a ton of rocks on my lap.

Melinda continued, "She told me, and I quote, 'They can't make you repent. Nobody can make you repent until you're ready. So, you might as well have a good time until you're ready to change.'"

What twisted rationale.

Oh, Carrie, I thought, you're fooling yourself! You're leading a double life—one lacking any integrity. You have grossly misunderstood the doctrine of repentance. Such enormous lies. Lies to school authorities. Lies to bishops. Most of all, lies to yourself.

Melinda brought me back to the room with her next statement. "Somebody needs to do something about this. I can't turn her in. I just can't do that. But somebody needs to do something to stop her. Somebody needs to get through to her before she gets into a bigger mess than she's already in. Only you can't talk to her, because she'll know I told you all this, so promise you'll just talk to the bishop at home. I think she really needs help."

I encouraged Melinda to talk openly with Carrie and to urge her to see her campus bishop.

"I'll talk to the bishop when I get home," I told her.

When I got home, I went to the bishop heavyhearted. I felt like a rat. I was involving myself in a chain of events that very likely could lead to Carrie's expulsion from BYU. After all, Carrie had signed a contract promising to live BYU's standards, and she had violated that contract. Her academic future was uncertain, but of greater consequence by far was her spiritual well-being. Carrie was following the course of the "father of all lies." She thought she was deceiving others, but she herself was the real victim, the victim of self-deceit. Maybe my talk with the bishop and any subsequent consequences would help to awaken her. Maybe she needed a shock to bring her to her senses. If she had any sense, which, at this point, I doubted.

Carrie's home bishop called Carrie's BYU bishop. None of this information was news to him. He had felt prompted to talk to her, and two other young people who were gravely concerned about Carrie's spiritual welfare had already come to him, as well. He called Carrie in to talk to him.

No, there was nothing bothering her. Yes, she was obeying the commandments. No, she didn't feel the need to discuss anything with him. No, nothing was awry in her life. Again she had lied.

He felt she was lying and lovingly questioned her again, but she did not alter her story.

The end of the semester approached, and Carrie came home for the summer. We didn't see her in church much; on the occasions when I did run into her, she was obviously uncomfortable.

When September rolled around, Carrie did not return to BYU. All her partying had affected her grades, and she had failed to make sufficient academic progress to register again. Knowing that, she did not take her continuing endorsement papers to her home bishop.

I never see much of Carrie anymore. I think she actively avoids her old church friends. She's told ward members that she's attending the young adult branch, but I don't think she really does. I've inquired about her, and others who are active in that branch have told me that they never see her. They tell me she has a job that requires her to work on Sundays.

More lies. The truth is, Carrie isn't attending the young adult branch. Though she does work on Sunday, it isn't required. Another young Latter-day Saint woman works with her and manages to get Sundays off with little hassle.

How I wish that Carrie could just tell the truth! I wish she could face the truth. I wish Carrie could simply say, "I'm not attending church anymore." At least that truth would be a start for her.

I find myself thinking about Carrie a lot, wondering what I could have done for her. Was there something else I could have said or done? Is there something I can do for her now?

I see other young people like Carrie who don't feel that telling the truth is important, who feel that lies are "little things." I ache for them and try to warn them about the dangerous path of lies. I try to teach the important principle of honesty—especially honesty with yourself.

Carrie was right about one thing: no one can make her repent. She won't let anyone get close enough to really help her. So, I pray for her, and I worry about her, this prisoner of lies, for I know that the words of Solomon are true: "He that covereth his sins shall not prosper: but whoso confesseth and forsaketh them shall have mercy" (Proverbs 28:13).

I hope that someday Carrie will choose to change. I hope that Carrie, as well as my other young friends who find the path of lies beguiling, will cease to be duped by the greatest deceiver of all. I hope and pray that they will choose to move towards spiritual prosperity by selecting another path—a path of mercy, light, . . . and truth.

Bring Him Back

Ye must watch and pray always lest ye enter into temptation; for Satan desireth to have you, that he may sift you as wheat. Therefore ye must always pray unto the Father in my name.
— *3 Nephi 18:18–19*

Ron hurdled his back fence and ran down the quiet residential street as fast as his lean sprinter's legs would take him. Even after five years, that picture of him remains in my memory as if it were a photograph snapped and filed within easy reach. His gray sweats were tucked into untied, high-top basketball shoes, and his maroon windbreaker flapped behind him. He didn't look back—he just kept running down the road at a pace too fast for me to follow until he disappeared around a curve. I shivered as I watched him go and then went back into Ron's house.

Kris, Ron's mother, sat slumped over the kitchen table. Her sobbing had subsided to low moans, each followed by a noisy inhalation of air. I put my arms around her. "Did he hit you?" I asked. She had called me in a panic, saying she was in danger. I'd driven to Kris's house immediately.

She shook her head no. Good. I was afraid he had. Ron, when he was angry, was capable of doing anything.

"I'm sorry I couldn't stop him, but he ran so fast. I'll call the police, okay? Maybe they can pick him up."

She nodded.

Ron had a history of running away. He had a drug history, too: he'd used, bought, dealt, and stolen. He had dropped out of high school.

Kris had been a widow since Ron was eight, when her husband died of cancer. She had tried everything to help Ron change when she'd learned of his drug addiction: she'd sent him to live with relatives, she had enrolled him in youth rehabilitation programs, and she had worked with him in family therapy.

Ron's behavior had sometimes improved for short spurts of time, and he'd returned to school. But recently he had been kicked out again. His last stunt was stealing Kris's credit cards to purchase things he could sell quickly to raise money for his habit. Furthermore, some ward members suspected him of breaking into their houses and stealing their possessions.

I called the police to give a brief report, and they promised to send a unit over. Kris lifted her head and wiped her eyes and nose.

"He'll be back, Kris. He's just angry. Maybe the police will find him. He can't be very far away."

Ron was supposed to enter a special wilderness survival program for troubled kids that next morning. Supposed to. Empty words, powerless against Ron's rage and will. My husband, Scott, after counseling with Ron for months, had arranged it. But now Ron had thrown a fit, accosted his mother, and disappeared over the fence, leaving his stereo, clothes, and camping equipment strewn across the backyard where he'd angrily tossed them from his bedroom window.

I felt acutely responsible for Ron's running away this time. I'd confronted him, tried to calm him down, and failed. The moment I told him I was calling the police if he gave us more trouble, he'd dropped his things and leapt over the fence.

The police did not find Ron, and he didn't return home that night. I hardly slept, worrying about his safety and feeling responsible for his flight. The next day, we waited anxiously for word from Ron, but none came. He didn't call. He didn't return home. None of his friends had seen him.

Days turned into weeks. Scott and I hunted for Ron, assisted by a group of concerned friends in the ward. We involved teenagers from the ward, following their tips to all the local hangouts and hideouts. We left messages with dozens of people to call if they saw Ron anywhere. Finally, after two weeks, some kids told us that they'd seen Ron near the high school. Others soon reported that they'd seen him in a nearby park. It was a relief to know he was still in the area. But no one could take us to him.

Then Steve, the priests quorum adviser, called, and our worries mounted. His son, a policeman, knew of a drug operation in our neighborhood that involved a house where, according to one of the kids in the ward, Ron occasionally stayed. If the police arrested the occupants of the house while Ron was there, he would go to prison for a long time because he had just passed his eighteenth birthday and would be prosecuted as an adult. A thin and handsome kid, we feared what would happen to Ron if he landed in prison.

That night Scott and one of Ron's young friends searched for Ron until three in the morning. When Scott came home, alone, I'd never seen him look so dejected. "We can't find him," he said, his voice shaking with emotion. "We've looked everywhere. I've been in every dive in this town, walked around every single park, and checked out every twenty-four-hour restaurant. Nobody knows where he is. I don't know what else we can do."

Worried, I too had not slept. I climbed out of bed, where I'd been reading, and rubbed my husband's tired neck and shoulder muscles as he sat on the edge of the bed, his head in his hands. Seeing his frustration and anguish, I felt my own heart breaking. Scott had done everything he could for Ron. He knew how Ron ached for adult male companionship and how hard it was for him to be a teenager without his own father near. Scott had tried to fill that void and had urged other men in the ward to reach out to Ron as well.

"We've done everything we can do, honey," I said. "I guess all we can do now is pray."

Together we knelt, held each other's hands, and asked God to bring Ron back. We prayed that if Larry, Ron's father, could help, that he could attend to his son, since Ron was seemingly beyond our earthly reach. We also prayed that something would happen to change Ron's heart and that he'd come home, so we could all try to help him one more time.

Exhausted, we climbed into bed and eventually fell asleep.

The next day, we arose, full of faith and expectation. We called Ron's home and asked if they'd received any news of Ron. They hadn't. We went through that day with thoughts of Ron and prayers for his safety running through our minds constantly. We began to doubt our prayers were being heard, yet we prayed for Ron again that night and fell asleep worried and depressed.

Was there something else we should have done? Some place we should have searched? Did we lack sufficient faith for divine intervention?

Early the next morning, the phone rang. It was Ron's sister. "Hi, Sister Bowen," she said. "Mom said to call and tell you that Ron's here."

"You mean he's at your house?" I couldn't believe my ears. I sent a quick, silent prayer heavenward. "Thank you, thank you, Heavenly Father." My heart was filled with relief and gratitude.

"Yeah. He's upstairs in his room asleep. He looks pretty hammered."

"When did he get there?"

"Sometime early this morning. Mom opened the front door to leave for work and found him crumpled in a ball on our porch. I think he's pretty sick."

That was an understatement. Ron was quite sick. In fact, he'd very nearly died.

Later Ron told us what had happened that day and night. He'd been with druggie friends freebasing cocaine, on top of using some other drugs, and had such a terrible physical reaction that he was certain he was going to die. He was more scared than he'd ever been in his life. Then he realized that he didn't want to die. Not like this. Not where he was.

He said a prayer. Even in his drugged state, he could think of doing that. It was a very short prayer, only four words, "Heavenly Father, help me!" He said that prayer repeatedly.

The only thing he could think of doing was to try to get as close to home as he could before his body stopped functioning. Luckily, he was in town, so there was a chance he could get home, if he could keep walking long enough.

He stumbled along the city streets, thinking only of getting closer to home with each step he took. He prayed continually, hoping that his heart would continue beating but doubting that it would.

He never knew how he made it to his mother's front door. When he got there, he didn't have the energy to knock or push the doorbell before he dropped, unable to move. Daylight was just breaking.

Kris found him on the front porch when she opened the door to go to work. She is a nurse and though she couldn't rouse Ron, she gave him a quick physical appraisal and felt that he was

probably okay. She called to her other children, and they dragged
Ron into the house and got him into bed. Ron slept, almost non-
stop, for two days.

After that frightening night, Ron again agreed to let Scott try
to help him. Scott again enrolled Ron in the wilderness program.
This time, Ron packed his stuff, allowed Scott to put him on a
plane, and went through a rigorous one-month program in the
Arizona desert.

He admits, now, that if he'd known what he was in for, he
never would have walked onto that plane. But when he did in fact
survive the month, he knew he could do anything. And he knew
that God would help him. Anytime. Anywhere.

When Ron returned from Arizona, he enrolled in an out-
patient drug program at a local hospital and regularly attended
Alcoholics Anonymous meetings. He came back to church, and
kept coming. He made new, straight friends and participated in
church youth programs. He got a job, and kept it. He enrolled in
courses at the community college.

When Ron successfully passed the high school equivalency
exam, we celebrated by taking him out for dinner. At dinner, he
asked my husband if he could serve a mission in the future, if he
could stay straight and earn the money to go.

The changes Ron made did not come easily. Hour by hour,
he fought his addictions, and he began turning his life around.
Soon, the hours stretched to days, and then to weeks, and then
to months.

At the end of a year, we watched Ron board another plane.
This time, he was dressed in a white shirt and a dark suit and
was headed on a mission. He'd been clean for more than a year.
He'd worked hard to save the money to finance his mission. He
was filled with the Spirit and anxious to serve the Lord.

Ron served an honorable mission, working very hard. He had

many successes, but when the work did not go well or he had trouble with a companion, he fell into depressions and felt the old craving to lose himself in a drugged stupor. Through prayer and self-discipline, however, he refused to give in to those feelings. The Lord brought him through those tough times.

It would be wonderful to sign off this story with a happy-ever-after ending at this point. Unfortunately, that's not what happened.

We were thrilled to greet Ron when he got home from his mission. His family had been greatly blessed during his mission service, and they looked forward to having him home with them, his younger brother in particular. His mother and sisters were excited about having a returned missionary in their midst.

Ron was okay for a while. He found a good job, he enrolled in school, and he served in the ward, working with the youth.

Then one day he didn't show up at work, and he didn't come home. Ron seemed to disappear off the face of the earth.

Kris feared that Ron had succumbed to his old addictions. Her fears were confirmed when Ron called to tell Kris that he would not be coming home. He'd run into his old friends. He'd found the temptation to "take a hit" too great to overcome, and he'd spent a night doing drugs. He'd stayed for another night and then another.

Ron's experience confirmed what all the drug and alcohol literature claims: it had taken only one time to end up back where he'd started—his addictions were now ruling his body and he was back at the proverbial square one.

He was devastated and depressed. He felt there was no hope for him. He'd sinned against greater knowledge. He lacked the power to overcome his addictions. He just didn't have it in him to fight one more time. He was giving up and giving in.

We were heartsick and helpless. What could we do to help Ron now? We couldn't kidnap him. We couldn't force him into a rehabilitation program. We couldn't even reach him. He'd call Kris to report in, every now and then, but he wouldn't leave a number where he could be reached. He told Kris that he didn't want to talk to us.

We were devastated. I'd find myself thinking about Ron and wind up in tears. How could this have happened? Could I have done something to prevent it?

After talking with Kris and other close friends, we again concluded that all we could do for Ron was to pray for him.

Once again, we prayed fervently for Ron's health and safety and for divine assistance. Those thoughts became part of every prayer said in our home. Each time we went to the temple, we put Ron's name on the prayer roll. Others did those things as well. The ward fasted in Ron's behalf.

Nothing changed, except Ron started dropping by his home for short visits every now and then. These were bittersweet reunions for Kris and the other children. Ron sometimes went home when Kris wasn't there to beg for food or money from his sisters. He still avoided our home and the homes of his other Church friends.

One Sunday, months later, I was sitting in sacrament meeting when thoughts of him again pressed themselves upon my mind. Where was he? How was he doing?

The thoughts would not go away. All through sacrament meeting, my mind drifted to memories of Ron, and I felt the familiar concern and love for him rise in me. I felt an urgency to find him again. I prayed for Ron, but this time I added, "Heavenly Father, I just want to put my arms around Ron one more time and tell him I love him. That's all I want to do. Please, if it be thy will, bring him back."

That night I couldn't sleep because of thoughts of Ron. I

wondered if the Spirit was telling me something. I had no way of contacting Ron. All I could do was pray.

The next morning, I prayed again, still feeling the pressing need to find Ron and to put my arms around him. The feelings scared me. Was something going to happen to him? Was I wanting to say good-bye? Why was I having this constant train of thoughts about Ron? Were they promptings?

I went through my normal, busy, Monday routine. That afternoon, I decided to make a quick trip to the grocery store between my kids' piano lessons.

I grabbed the grocery list and headed to the store.

On this Monday afternoon, I'd worked my way through most of the aisles when I found myself wondering if I needed peanut butter. I decided I couldn't be bothered to go back to the peanut butter aisle, so I made a note to check the food storage peanut butter before my next shopping trip.

I rolled my cart about five feet when a voice inside my head said, "Go get some peanut butter."

I told myself I didn't have time. I needed to get through the aisles and check out, in order to meet the piano lesson schedule. Again I pushed the cart a few feet down the aisle. This time the voice insisted, "You need to go find the peanut butter." I looked around to see who was talking to me. No one was there.

I felt a little stupid, but I decided I'd better do what the voice said. I whipped the cart around and went to the peanut butter aisle. It was empty. I checked the peanut butter prices and found them too high: I'd wait for a sale. I was about to leave the aisle, wondering what the voice had been all about, when someone tapped me on the shoulder. I nearly jumped out of my skin. I turned around, and there stood Ron.

I threw my arms around him. He was skinny as a stick and

looked haggard and worn. There was no light in his eyes, and he was jumpy and nervous. But he hugged me back.

"Oh, Ron!" I told him, "It's so good to see you! You've been on my mind constantly for the last two days, and I've been praying that I'd find you somewhere."

Ron was startled. I was afraid he'd bolt, so I hugged him again. This time, I told him I'd been wanting to find him just to tell him how much I loved him.

With my words, Ron's countenance softened. He started to speak, and for the next twenty minutes, he poured out his heart to me. He spared no details and answered my questions with brutal honesty.

He'd been dealing drugs to support his own habit. He was pretty sure he was also an alcoholic by now, since he could down a fifth of liquor without any noticeable effect on his body.

He'd quit his job. He'd been feeling that he needed to get away from our city and that he needed to do it soon. The previous night, he'd been pulled over, and he'd thought he'd be arrested, but for some reason, the policeman let him go. That morning, he'd packed up all his things and decided to start driving until he felt like stopping. He'd come into the store to buy some food. He had a loaf of bread and a jar of jam in his hands. He was looking for soup. The soup shelves were across the aisle from the peanut butter.

"I can't believe you're here," he told me. "When I came to get the soup, I did a double take. Is that Sister Bowen? I asked myself. No, that's too weird. You see, I've been debating coming up to your house all day today. I remembered the way we used to talk to each other, and I thought you'd maybe help me sort this all out and help me decide what to do." It seemed as though he couldn't talk fast enough, and I didn't interrupt him.

"Yesterday, I realized that every single person I started to do drugs with all those years ago is either dead or in jail. I know that sounds unreal, but it's true. I'm the only one who's free, if you can call this free," he pointed to his skinny frame. "I know this is going to sound really strange, but I think my life has been preserved, for some reason. When the cop let me go last night, I was sure of it. Does that seem weird to you?" he asked.

He didn't give me time to answer, so I simply shook my head. No, it didn't seem weird to me, not at all.

"Then I thought about Alma the Younger and the sons of Mosiah. They were doing really bad things, but because of Alma's prayers, their lives were preserved and they were stopped in their tracks. And, I thought, maybe that was happening to me. Maybe God's giving me one more chance. What do you think?"

I told him that he'd always reminded me of Alma the Younger and that I knew many people who had been praying for him. I also told him I was sure God would be happy to give him one more chance, but it would be up to him to take it — or leave it.

We talked about his options and his plans, as we stood there in the peanut butter aisle. I knew one of my kids was missing a piano lesson, but I didn't mind. I'd explain later.

Ron couldn't stop talking. He seemed to be thinking out loud, and he shared his frustrations, fears, and sadness with me. I listened, all the while sending prayers heavenward. "Heavenly Father, thank you, thank you, thank you, for answering my prayer. Thank you for letting me hug Ron one more time. Please, please, please help me to say the right thing, to do the right thing. Please, please, please, let us have the Spirit here with us. Help me to do thy will. Help me to help Ron."

"I've been sort of thinking about calling a friend in California and maybe driving down there," Ron offered. "He's the father of an old girlfriend, and he told me once that if I ever decided to go straight, he'd let me live with him. He'll give me three months in his home to get some help, if I want to try again. Thing is, I'm not sure I can do it. I'm not sure I have it in me to work that hard to fight this. I'm so afraid of failing. I already hate myself."

Again, I put my arms around Ron, hugging him. People were passing us in the aisle, but I didn't care. "You can do this, Ron. I know you can, if you *decide* to do this. People are praying for you, and their prayers are being heard. You won't be alone. Not for a second. I think you do need to get out of this city. I think you need to drive up to your house right now, say good-bye to your family, and tell them where you're going. Then, you need to call your friend in California and tell him you're taking him up on his offer. Then, you need to get in your car and start driving south. I'll escort you to Portland, if you want me to, just to help you get on your way."

"You're right," he whispered. "I know you're right. That's what I ought to do. You know what? I think I'm going to do it."

From the moment he'd made that decision, he was on fire. He couldn't get out of the store fast enough. He hugged me, saying, "Keep praying for me, will you? I'll need it." He took off, running down the aisle, swinging a loaf of bread, and holding a jar of jam and a can of soup.

I stood there by the peanut butter and watched him go, praying fervently for his safety, for his health, for his success in once again overcoming his addictions. He'd succeeded once. I hoped he could succeed again.

I didn't know if I'd ever get to see Ron again. But at least I'd had the chance to put my arms around him one more time. I'd had the opportunity to tell him that I loved him.

Twice my prayers concerning Ron have been answered. Twice God has brought him back.

I'm still praying for him.

Your Countenance Shows

But your iniquities have separated between you and your God.

— Isaiah 59:2

I didn't know Meredith at all. In fact, I didn't know many of the teenagers in this new ward.

When my family had relocated months before, the bishop called me into the Relief Society presidency—a new experience for me, working with adults. I was surprised by my joy in the calling: I'd thought I'd suffer from being separated from the youth. In fact, I thought the bishop had made a big mistake—but I was wrong. Service with the sisters of the ward proved to be refreshing and nurturing.

I have to admit, however, that I envied my husband a little. He'd been called as the Young Men's president and priests quorum adviser. I'd been teaching young men and young women for years, and now he was lucky enough to work with them. I had to remind myself that the kids in this ward were not part of my stewardship—they were his.

So, when Meredith first walked by me at church, and I found myself thinking, "That girl is in trouble," I told myself to stay out of it. That young woman and whatever was troubling her were none of my business. Besides, who was I to be getting spiritual signals about a complete stranger? I decided to ignore the feeling.

The next Sunday, however, I found myself looking for Meredith. She was there, all right. No change in her countenance. It wasn't that she looked like anything was wrong with her: she was a beautiful girl, immaculately groomed. It was just that her countenance looked flat—there was no light in her face. Again I thought, "This girl is in trouble."

Curiosity aroused, I watched her for a while, before the meeting started. She seemed to be friendly and well-liked, judging from the way she moved from group to group before finding her family and taking her seat.

I knew a little about her family from serving in the Relief Society presidency. I learned more about ward members each week, eager to get to know these people who, experience had taught me, would soon become beloved friends. Meredith's parents were strong members of the ward: they'd served in leadership positions, many of them youth-oriented.

Well, I told myself, if Meredith is in trouble, then her parents are well equipped to deal with whatever it is. Besides, I don't know her. I've never even exchanged two words with her. I'll stay out of it.

Several weeks passed before I encountered Meredith again. This time I was shocked: she looked much worse. In fact, I would say that her countenance looked "dark." I wanted to reach out to her, to say, "What's wrong? Do you need somebody to talk to?" but I felt foolish. Instead, I smiled at her and simply said, "Hello."

She smiled back in response, but her smile did not light up her face.

During the sacrament, I prayed for Meredith, that she'd get some help. Then I asked Heavenly Father to clue me in about what was going on. Was I getting a spiritual prompting about Meredith's being in trouble? I didn't wait for an answer. Instead, I prayed that Meredith's parents would be aided in helping their daughter. I almost ended the prayer with, "Kindly leave me out of this," but I wasn't sure that "this" was anything real. Again I decided I should leave Meredith and her real or imagined troubles alone.

Another month went by. Meredith's countenance did not change. It was still dark. I watched some of the other girls her age: the comparison was revealing. Though I knew none of the girls, I could easily see an inner glow shining from most of them. Meredith, in contrast, looked like a dark cloud. Surely, those around her had seen it and moved to help.

I decided to ask my husband about her.

"What do you know about Meredith?" I asked.

"What prompts that question?"

"Oh, I just noticed her at church," I replied.

"Well," Scott thought a minute, "I know that she's popular at school. I know that she has a terrific family. I know that she's very nice looking. That's about it. Why?"

I hesitated. "It's probably nothing, but it seems to me that maybe something's wrong with her."

"Like what?" my husband asked.

"I have no idea. Every time I see her I've been getting funny feelings that she's in some kind of trouble. I know that sounds silly, because I don't even know her, but I keep getting those feelings. It's really none of my business—forget I asked."

Scott stared at me. "I can't just forget that you've asked. You've brought it up, and so now I'm thinking about it."

"Well, maybe you can ask Meredith's mother about her."

"Okay, I'll ask her," he replied.

Satisfied that I'd "done something," I let the subject drop. I didn't ask Scott about Meredith again. I really didn't want to hear what he'd have to say.

A few months later, our ward was reorganized, and we faced new callings and challenges when Scott was called to serve as bishop.

The next Sunday I ran into Meredith again. I tried to speak with her, but she was in a hurry. I did have the chance to look her straight in the eye as she passed. Darkness. Again, I felt the overwhelming feeling that something was definitely wrong.

That night, after Scott returned from long organizational meetings, we spent a few minutes together, talking and planning. Using the ward list to review ward members' names and consider special needs, we came upon the names of Meredith's family.

Again, I felt a prompting. This time, I was sure that the Spirit was trying to tell me something. This time, there was a stewardship to consider.

"Honey, you need to talk to Meredith," I said. "I don't know why, but you do."

"I know," Scott replied. "I was just thinking the same thing."

Scott added her name to a list of people he intended to interview. He never handed her name to his appointment secretary, however, because Meredith called two nights later, saying, "Bishop, can I come and talk to you?"

I don't know the details of that interview. I do know that the promptings were based on real need. I know that because, many months later, Meredith's mother confided in me. Meredith was in big spiritual trouble. She had made some bad choices.

Because of those choices, whatever they were, the Spirit had ceased to accompany her. Her inner light was gone.

I tell this story for a couple of reasons. First of all, to illustrate a lesson I learned personally—that the Spirit prompts us to help others. It is up to us to act on the promptings, whether they relate to our formal stewardships or not. For months, I ignored prompt-ings about Meredith or chose not to act on them. I still have no idea why I received them. I can't waste time on that question. The fact remains that the Spirit was trying to move me to action.

The greater questions are these: What could I have done for Meredith? How might I have helped her? What could have been prevented by surer and swifter action or intervention? I'll never know the answers to those questions, but I do know this: I should have acted on those promptings.

The second reason I tell this story is that our countenances reveal a great deal about us. If we are living righteously, there is light within us and about us. That light shines, particularly from our eyes. Conversely, if our iniquities have separated us from God, there is a void. Often, there is darkness.

I know from personal experience that if I trust in and act on the whisperings of the Spirit, I can be an instrument in the Lord's hand. I also know that our countenances reveal much about us and our lives. A wise teacher uses that information to teach, instruct, and lift. Over time, I have been fortunate enough to see many a dark countenance return to light.

Meredith's was one of them.

Forgiving

> *He that forgiveth not his brother his trespasses standeth condemned before the Lord; for there remaineth in him the greater sin. I, the Lord, will forgive whom I will forgive, but of you it is required to forgive all men.*
> *— Doctrine & Covenants 64:9–10*

"I don't do forgiveness," David said.

I winced. We were talking about a friend who had double-crossed him, and I'd said, "You might just have to forgive him."

David did not like that idea. He was hurt. He felt he couldn't trust his friend anymore. He was sure they could never be friends again.

"Ah, David, that statement tells me how young you are. I'm fairly certain you'll find you won't be able to survive in this life without 'doing' forgiveness."

"I'm sorry. You know me—if you hurt me, that's it. I just don't do forgiveness."

David's statement stayed with me for days. I thought of times that David himself had been forgiven. Given enough time, David would remember those occasions and come to understand this important principle. Sooner or later he would learn to "do" forgiveness.

I also thought about the times when I had experienced

firsthand how difficult it is to truly forgive those who have wronged us.

Alex was a bright, talented young man who lived in my ward. He had a great sense of humor. He was also sensitive, and I knew from conversations we had that he had a tender heart.

I enjoyed a rewarding relationship with Alex's mother, Marilyn, too. She was a wonderful woman—intelligent, well-read, funny, and outspoken. A convert to the Church, she had a strong testimony of the gospel and always served diligently, often in leadership callings.

Unfortunately, Marilyn's marriage was troubled. Eventually those troubles led to divorce, and the months leading to the divorce were fraught with suffering for everyone involved.

Through that time, I remained close to both Marilyn and Alex. Often when they had disputes, Marilyn would ask me to talk to Alex, or he would come on his own, seeking a sympathetic ear. I tried to help him negotiate a new relationship with his father and his mother. We talked a lot about his relationships with his girlfriend and his boyfriends. Mostly, I listened to him. Occasionally I'd give him some advice.

I invested in Alex considerable time, energy, love, and prayer. He was a kid in crisis, and this was a pivotal year for him. Besides handling the business of finishing high school and preparing for college, Alex was trying to pick his way through relationships that were mined with difficulties, complications, and implications. I wanted to help see him across those treacherous mine fields.

The decision to be a friend to both Alex and Marilyn often left me in the tricky position of playing between them, but I promised them both that I would keep their confidences, and I did. I'd carefully answer questions, or give my opinion or advice when I was asked. Occasionally, I'd have to reply, "You know I can't tell you that," or, "You two need to work this out."

Sometimes, I'd be the advocate for one or the other; often, I'd act as a bridge between them. Mother and son loved each other deeply and wanted to survive this difficult time with that love intact.

Alex graduated from high school. He was headed toward BYU in the fall and was excited about being on his own. Through the summer, Alex regularly dropped by my house or called when he needed me, and I continued to visit frequently with Marilyn. At the end of the summer, Alex left for Provo. Though he was scarred by the family's problems, I was confident he would thrive at BYU.

Throughout the semester, I'd hear from him or about him. Marilyn often read me Alex's letters or called to tell me about their Sunday night phone calls. Alex was a little homesick, which was gratifying to his mother. His frequent expressions of love and appreciation were balm for her wounded soul. I was thrilled to see the healing process in each of them.

At Christmastime, Alex returned home. We spent a beautiful Christmas Eve together, and a fine spirit of love filled our home that night. Alex promised to come by again during the holidays.

Several days later Alex phoned. He was obviously upset, and he told me he was calling from the bus station. He and his mother had fought, he said, and he wasn't going to stay around for any more of it. He was returning to Provo early.

I tried to talk him out of those plans. Surely, he and Marilyn could resolve their differences if he'd stay here. I didn't want him returning to school to spend a lonely week in the dorms, especially with an unpleasant memory lodged in his brain, and I knew how much Marilyn would be hurt by Alex's sudden departure. I talked like crazy, trying to keep him from boarding that bus.

Finally, he said, "Sister Bowen, I know you're trying to help, but I've got to go. They're calling my bus right now, so I've got to hang up. No, there isn't time for you to come down here to talk to me. I've made up my mind. The one thing you can do for me is to call my mother and tell her what I've told you. I tried to call, but I couldn't get through."

The line went dead. I quickly located the bus terminal phone number and called. The bus for Salt Lake had not left yet. I had Alex paged. He didn't answer.

I dialed Marilyn's number. She answered immediately. Surprised, I asked her if she had just come home, and she told me that she'd been home all morning.

"Have you been on the phone? Or have you had the answering machine taking calls?"

"No, why?" Marilyn asked.

I told her why.

"He left?" she whispered.

"I think so. I had him paged, and he didn't answer."

She was devastated. "He'd written such lovely letters, and I thought that, at last, we would be friends again."

When I got off the phone, I cried for my two friends.

Throughout the week until school resumed again in Provo, Marilyn and I tried to reach Alex, to assure him that, no matter what, he was loved. We could not find him.

Finally, Marilyn called Alex's father. He was perplexed, because Alex had told him he was spending the week with friends. He hadn't seen him.

Two months went by. Alex did not call home on Sunday nights. Marilyn was hurt so badly that she didn't call either. Alex did write, though his letters were short and painfully newsy—the kind of letters you write to a mere acquaintance.

In February I ran into one of Alex's friends at a basketball game. We chatted throughout the ball game, and eventually we came around to the topic of Alex.

"Yeah," Kent said, "that was a mess. It made me really mad the way he lied to you."

I felt a little zing. "What do you mean?" I asked.

"Well, you know how Alex set up that bus depot thing and had you call and lie to his mom and everything."

My face must have registered my dismay, because Kent stopped talking and said, "Oh, wow, you mean you still don't know about this?"

I shook my head. "I don't know about any set-up or lies. Why don't you enlighten me?"

Kent squirmed. "Man, I don't want to be stuck in the middle of this. I'm sorry, but I'm not going to tell you anything else. I just can't."

Kent would not say another word. In fact, he went to find another seat, so I couldn't ask him more questions.

I fretted and fumed. Had Alex really involved me in a set-up? The news I'd broken to Marilyn that day nearly wiped her out. I was very angry at the thought that Alex had double-crossed us both.

When I got home, I called another of Alex's friends and asked him what Alex had done during the second week of Christmas vacation.

"Oh, he was around here. He had that big fight with his mom, you know, so he made it look like he'd left town, but he didn't really leave. He stayed with friends in another ward. Then he drove back to Utah with the people he'd always planned to drive with. Why?" he wondered.

"I was curious. I've been worrying about him."

I was extremely angry. Alex had been intentionally deceitful, and he'd used me, unwittingly, to lie to Marilyn, my dear friend.

Now I was in another quandary. Should I tell Marilyn what I knew?

My husband urged me to tell Marilyn. "She's entitled to know. Besides, sooner or later, she's going to find out, because it's obvious that many people know that Alex was here that week."

It took me days to get up the nerve to call Marilyn. I needed to cool down. Alex had betrayed me. I had invested so much of myself in him, and he'd turned on me. He'd lied to me, and he'd used me to lie for him. I was hurt and I was angry.

When I called Marilyn, we had a tearful conversation. She was not shocked because she'd heard some things, but she hadn't yet added it all up: a neighbor had mentioned seeing Alex on New Year's Eve; a ward member had thought she'd seen him at a store; Alex's friends avoided Marilyn and generally acted "fishy." Now she understood.

I apologized to her for my part in the whole ordeal. She replied that I couldn't have known that I was actually lying—there was "nothing to forgive," as far as I was concerned.

Her words struck me. Forgive. That was my next task, I knew. I'd have to get over my anger and my hurt, and I'd have to forgive Alex. I knew what the scriptures said about that.

It was easier said than done. For weeks, every time I thought of Alex, anger would rise within me. He'd be home in April. I'd surely see him then, and what would I do about this?

I decided to do nothing. Marilyn confronted Alex, and they began to communicate again. Yes, Alex knew that I knew about the whole mess. He wondered if I were angry with him.

I admired Marilyn for the way she handled this problem. I was still avoiding Alex. I still felt hurt and betrayed.

April rolled around, and the grapevine brought news that Alex was home. He didn't come to see me.

I prayed that I would be able to forgive him, that I could

remove the hard shell that encased my heart whenever I heard his name.

The Lord must have heard that prayer, because three days later Alex was plopped down under my nose in a situation where I could not avoid him. We were having our house painted, and the contractor had hired Alex, of all people, to tape our windows.

I panicked. We had not spoken to each other since that December morning when he'd called me. As I watched him climb out of the car, I could see that Alex was every bit as nervous as I was about the inevitable meeting.

I stepped back from the window and retreated to my bedroom. "Heavenly Father, please help me to do the right thing with Alex. I know I should be able to forgive him, but I haven't been able to do that yet. Please soften my heart toward him. He did a very stupid thing, and it was wrong, but it has hurt me too much and too long. Please take away the anger and the hurt. Help me to move on. Help me to be loving. Help me to be kind."

The doorbell rang. I went to answer it. When I opened the door, Alex was at the bottom of the stairs, standing sideways, so he didn't have to look at me.

Time slowed to a turtle's pace. I knew Alex was waiting to see my reaction and would respond to my cue. He looked like a vulnerable little boy to me, not a young man preparing to go on a mission, and my heart softened immediately. I wanted to fly down the stairs and hug him.

Instead I smiled and said in my most enthusiastic voice, "Hello! I've been waiting for you."

Alex turned toward me, and after carefully studying my face, he smiled back. In an instant, we both knew that we would be able to put December behind us. We would become friends again.

I am still surprised by how long it took me to work through the forgiving process with Alex. When we are angry, or hurt, or betrayed, it is harder to forgive others than we think it will be. Still, none of us can afford to take David's naive stance. We can't decide that we "don't do forgiveness." If we hold on to hurt and anger and allow our hearts to harden and to remain that way, we damage our own souls.

I have learned from this and other incidents that it is my duty and obligation and blessing to forgive. I know the value of that sweet gift when it has been generously offered to me by loving family and friends. Most important, I have learned in a very real way that the Lord offers forgiveness to each of us. "Inasmuch as you have forgiven one another your trespasses, even so I, the Lord, forgive you" (D&C 82:1).

The Scriptures Instruct

*The Book of Mormon and the holy scriptures are given
of me for your instruction; and the power of my Spirit
quickeneth all things.*
— *Doctrine & Covenants 33:16*

It was a fabulous seminary class reunion for the three days
we shared in San Diego. Twelve of us were there, some from
great distances: one recently returned missionary drove all the
way across the United States to be there. Three others, younger
siblings of former students, asked if they could come, too, and
we told them they were welcome. Even Mark, who was not a
member of the Church but had always hung around with this
group "because there's just something about these guys," had
flown in from Florida to join us.

It had been five years since all of us had been together. I'd
moved to another state, as had five of my former students. Three
of the students had married in the temple and had children. Five
young men and one young woman had returned from missions.

The Thompsons generously let us use their home as a central
gathering place. We caught up on news, exchanged stories, reminisced, laughed, and cried. We had a barbecue and pool party at
a ward member's house, a memorial dinner at a restaurant in
honor of all the "bonus points" the kids had earned over the

years, and, of course, a beach picnic and surfing expedition, because this was the group who had included the daily surf report in the class business at the beginning of each seminary hour.

Every minute of the reunion was wonderful, but the highlight of the three days was the testimony meeting we held on Sunday night, when the students told about their spiritual odysseys of the past five years, and shared what they'd learned. The memory of that evening, and the light and love that filled the Thompsons' living room that night, will always stand out as one of the most joyous occasions of my life.

I particularly enjoyed observing the individual growth — spiritual, emotional, and physical — that the years had produced for my former students. Those who attended were in great shape, I felt — all except Dustin, one of the younger brothers.

Dustin had grown from a cute nine-year-old boy to a handsome, articulate seventeen-year-old. During the reunion, whenever I watched or talked with him, an alarm went off in my head. Dustin was floundering; he seemed to lack a testimony of the gospel; he was "going nowhere" at the moment and lacked a plan for his future. One of the returned missionaries confided to me that Dustin was struggling with some "personal problems" and seemed headed for trouble.

For those reasons, I was especially grateful that Dustin joined our group. During the days of the reunion he heard many great missionary stories, he witnessed kind acts of generosity and service, and he saw wholesome and supportive relationships modeled for him. In addition, he participated in numerous hours of good, clean fun.

These experiences worked together to plant a seed of change in his heart. He was particularly moved by the testimonies borne on Sunday night and said so.

When I hugged these dear friends good-bye, Dustin said, "I've kind of made a mess out of my life recently, and this experience with all of you has made a difference. It's meant a lot to me." Then he asked me if he could call me if he needed someone to talk to.

"Of course you can, if you can afford the long-distance charges," I teased. "Seriously, Dustin, please keep in touch. I want to know how you're doing, and what you decide to do with your future."

Before leaving, I asked two of the returned missionaries to stay close to Dustin, to include him in their activities, to listen to him, and to teach him what they'd learned about the gospel. They promised me they would do that, and they did.

I returned home to face the new challenge of being a bishop's wife and quickly learned to focus on another group of teenagers: those in my ward.

In September, a letter came from Dustin. He had decided he needed to get back in school. He had already completed all the work to be accepted and enrolled in BYU by January. "Boy, I'm happy you came down," he wrote. "I learned a lot from our short time together. I'm so excited about the Y. It feels so good to know what's going on and where I'm going. It's such a change from total confusion." Immensely pleased that Dustin was moving forward, I wrote back and told him so.

Several weeks later, Dustin called me. He had begun to study the scriptures again, and he was feeling terrible pangs of guilt. His voice was full of misery. He'd prayed but felt no relief.

I didn't know the specifics of his regrets, so I prayed fervently that Heavenly Father would guide my words and help me know what to say to help Dustin. As soon as I concluded my silent prayer, into my mind came this scripture reference: Alma 42. That was all. Alma 42. I couldn't remember what, exactly, was written in Alma 42, so I suggested that he get his scriptures out and turn to Alma 42 while I went to get mine.

When I returned to the phone, I flipped the pages of my Book of Mormon to Alma 42 and discovered that I had highlighted and cross-referenced verse 29, Alma's words of counsel to his son Corianton about repentance: "And now, my son, I desire that ye should let these things trouble you no more, and only let your sins trouble you, with that trouble which shall bring you down unto repentance."

I had cross-referenced this beautiful verse to Doctrine and Covenants 58:42–43, so I read that passage to Dustin as well: "Behold, he who has repented of his sins, the same is forgiven, and I the Lord, remember them no more. By this ye may know if a man repenteth of his sins—behold, he will confess them and forsake them."

Dustin and I talked for a long time about the repentance process. Through our conversation, it became clear to me that Dustin had not completely repented of some past wrongdoings. I encouraged him to make an appointment with his bishop.

Before hanging up, I suddenly felt a strong impression to tell Dustin to go back to the beginning of Alma's conversation with Corianton and read the whole account.

"Dustin," I said, "this may strike you as strange, but I feel an overwhelming impression to tell you to read Alma 39 through 42. Read all of it."

Dustin and I said our good-byes, and I hung up. Later that night, after my children were asleep, I returned to my Book of Mormon and read the chapters I'd asked Dustin to read. I hoped that account of a father speaking to a son would help him somehow.

Several months later, Dustin wrote to tell me what had happened to him that night. He'd found a quiet, secluded spot, and he'd read the chapters I'd asked him to read. He told me that every word had been enlightening to him and relevant. It was as though the Lord were talking straight to him. He'd never had an experience with the scriptures like it.

More important, these scriptures had pointed the way for him. Suddenly, he understood the repentance process and could begin to work his way through it. That was a significant turning point in his life, and he wanted to thank me for my part in it. "You know, I probably have a better testimony of your revelation than of anything else."

It wasn't my revelation, I wrote back. Plain and simple, I had received direction through the Holy Ghost when I'd prayed to say the right thing to help Dustin. That prayer had been answered with a scripture reference that registered strongly in my mind.

Dustin is not the only one who was helped that night. That valuable lesson has often been reinforced in my own life: when I have needed counsel, advice, comfort, or strength, I've often turned to my scriptures to find exactly what I needed. "But continue thou in the things which thou hast learned and hast been assured of, knowing of whom thou hast learned them. . . . Thou hast known the holy scriptures, which are able to make thee wise unto salvation through faith which is in Christ Jesus. All scripture is given by inspiration of God, and is profitable for doctrine, for reproof, for correction, for instruction in righteousness" (2 Timothy 3:14–16).

Lost and Found

What man of you, having an hundred sheep, if he lose one of them, doth not leave the ninety and nine in the wilderness, and go after that which is lost, until he find it? . . . And when he cometh home, he calleth together his friends and neighbors, saying unto them, Rejoice with me; for I have found my sheep which was lost.
— Luke 15:4, 6

Anyone who teaches teenagers knows of their vulnerability during those particularly tempestuous years. Teachers and leaders and parents know that no matter how hard they work and how fiercely they love, some of these precious "sheep" are kept in the flock, some are brought back in, and, sadly, others are lost.

I've witnessed my share of wandering sheep, and, unfortunately, I've seen many sheep wander off so far that they seem to have been lost from the flock of the Church.

These sheep may be lost, but they are not forgotten. I wonder about them and worry about them: where is Cory? Robin? Tom? Bonnie? John? Shawn? Chuck? Debbie? Jerry? Many former students have moved beyond my reach, and I don't know where to find them. I often pray that those near them will reach out to them, support them, and love them.

Late, late one night, or, I should say, early, early one morning, the phone rang. As the phone rang again, my husband awakened and moaned, "I hate these middle-of-the night calls."

"I know," I muttered back, as I reached for the phone.

"Hello?" I tried not to sound too sleepy.

"Hello! Annette?"

The male voice stirred a memory in the far reaches of my brain. "Yes?" I responded.

"Guess who this is!"

This man sounded way too cheerful for this hour of the morning, and I did not want to play any silly Guess Who? games. Still, I didn't want to be rude, so I said, "Say something else. Your voice is familiar, but I can't quite place it."

"Okay. I'll give you a hint . . . "

That was all he needed to say. Suddenly, the identity of this voice and the handsome young man it belonged to zoomed up out of my memory bank.

"Richard?" I asked, my voice reflecting my surprise. I had not seen or heard from Richard in seven years, ever since he moved away from our ward.

"Yes! I knew you'd remember me! I told my wife that I could call you any time, day or night, and you'd know who I was." He spoke to someone who was obviously in the room with him, "I told you! She knew who I was; so there!"

I was glad my memory had served me so well.

"Where are you, Richard?" I was fully awake now and ready to ask intelligent questions.

My husband rustled in the darkness. "Richard who?" he mumbled.

I turned on my reading light, grabbed a paper and pencil, and wrote out Richard's name. Scott squinted at the paper, waiting for his eyes to adjust to the light, and then raised his eyebrows in surprise.

Richard told me that he was in Hawaii. It was a few minutes past 11:00 P.M., his time, and he and his wife had just returned from having dinner at the home of mutual friends.

He told me that he was a military policeman and that he'd recently run into Brother Kellermann on base. They had both been surprised to see each other thousands of miles and seven years away from the time when we'd all been in the same ward together. Brother Kellermann had written down Richard's name and number and promised to call.

"I didn't think he'd really call back," Richard said. "You know how it is. You run into someone you used to know and you promise to get together, but then no one does anything about it. So, when Brother Kellermann called back this week and invited my wife and me to dinner, I went into shock. I told him about my little kids and said I'd have a hard time getting a babysitter, but he just said, 'Bring them with you! We want to meet them.' My wife was kinda surprised. Anyway, we went over there tonight, and it was so cool. They loved the kids, and we all had a great time. My wife isn't a member of the Church, and she doesn't know much about it, since I never go, and I worried a bit about how things would be. But it was great. We all loved it."

"The Kellermanns are wonderful people," I said.

"Yeah, they're the best," he agreed. "Anyway, we were talking about old times and people we both knew, and that's when I found out that they still keep in touch with you and that they had your phone number. I made them write it down for me. I was so excited that I called you the minute we stepped back in our house!"

I decided not to mention the time difference between Hawaii and the West Coast.

We had a long conversation. I learned about Richard's work, his wife, and his three children. He asked me for news of mutual acquaintances and old friends. Toward the end of the conversation, I again expressed my amazement that he would call me after all these years. I told him that I'd often thought about him and had wondered where he was and what he was doing. In fact, I explained, I had tried to track him down through some other friends.

"Yeah, well, I've been missing you," he said.

"I've been missing you." The sweetness of this simple, tender declaration stirred my heart. I could feel the old love between us, despite the passage of years and the distance of miles.

Richard continued, "It's been seven years, but I've thought about you a lot, and remembered all the good times we had in that seminary class, and the mornings when you'd send someone over to get me when I didn't show up."

Then there was silence on the line, as we both remembered those mornings. Another student had a moped, and when Richard didn't show up, he'd go rouse Richard and haul him over to class.

"Let me tell you something," Richard's voice quivered a bit. "Being in the Kellermanns' home tonight reminded me of some of the things I've been missing." Another long pause.

I waited to hear what he'd say next.

"I guess I ought to do something about it," he sighed.

"Yes, you should," I encouraged.

Thank heaven for the Kellermanns, I thought. Thank heaven for that chance encounter on a military base in Hawaii. Thank heaven Brother Kellermann had been true to his word and had extended hospitality to this "lost sheep." Thank heaven for the Spirit that filled the Kellermann home. Maybe, just maybe, that experience would motivate Richard to "do something about" what he was missing in his life.

Before we hung up, Richard said, "Hey, I forgot to tell you something all those years ago."

I could tell that he felt a little awkward, for he hesitated a minute, and I wondered what the something might be.

"You meant a lot to me back then," he continued. "You might not think so, but you really made a difference in my life. I wasn't lying when I said that I think about you all the time. And I love you."

The tears spilled up and over and trickled down my face. "I love you, too, Richard," I responded.

"Yeah. I know you do."

It's been another five years since that phone call. Though Richard kept me posted for a while about his family's activities, he has made one too many moves without sending me a new address, and I've lost him again.

I often pray that wherever Richard is (as well as my other lost friends), there are people like the Kellermanns who share their love and lives freely and will reach out to bring Richard and other "lost sheep" back to the fold.

I also hope that there are people who will not give up on them. Janette was the one who taught me this valuable lesson, when I had practically given up on her.

I taught Janette for years. I knew of her struggles. I had watched the cycle many times: she'd make a stupid mistake; she'd be angry; she'd blame others and find fault with anyone and everyone; eventually she'd turn the hate towards herself; then she'd decide she wasn't worth anything; so, she'd go make another stupid mistake. Around she'd go again. Occasionally, she would make real progress in overcoming bad habits or pulling herself up out of the hole she'd dug for herself, but then, wham, she would start the cycle again.

It seemed to me that Janette was like a missile set on self-destruct. I and others around her listened to her, counseled with her, shored her up, cheered for her, and prayed for inner strength, heavenly love, and divine assistance for her. But nothing seemed to work.

After several years of the pattern, I had decided to throw in the proverbial towel. Janette wore me out. If she wanted to be so blind, so stupid, and so rebellious, she could do it on her own. I wanted out of the friendship.

I allowed our relationship to cool. I needed the emotional space. I knew I couldn't change Janette—only she could make the decisions to change—and, after years of time and experience, I doubted that I could do anything more to help her or influence her positively.

I announced to my husband, "I've given up on Janette." I explained, "She's never going to change. I think she wants to be unhappy. So, let her be unhappy! Let her be stupid. But she can do it without my having to watch it all. I'm tired of the whole thing."

Luckily, I did not say any of that to Janette.

Several weeks later, the bishop asked Janette to speak in sacrament meeting.

"Big mistake," I said to my husband.

He wisely said, "It will be interesting to hear what she has to say."

As long as I live, I will never forget that sacrament meeting talk. It was beautifully prepared and eloquently delivered. Obviously, Janette had invested many hours of thought and prayer in preparing the talk.

As she spoke, I could tell instantly that she had reached a turning point in her life: she had experienced the "mighty change of heart" that Alma wrote about. "Have ye spiritually been born of God? Have ye received his image in your countenances? Have ye experienced this mighty change in your hearts?" (Alma 5:14).

Something had happened to Janette, and I was certain that at last she could answer yes to Alma's questions.

Janette spoke about reaching out to others, to help them "get found." She talked about never giving up on a person. She named the people in the ward who had not given up on her and expressed her love and appreciation for those people.

I was one of the people Janette named, and I felt terribly unworthy of her praise or thanks. I *had* given up on her. I knew it, my husband knew it, and the Lord knew it. At that moment, I promised that I would never give up on a lost sheep again.

I've kept that promise and have lived to see many turning points, many mighty changes of heart, and many moments of rejoicing as friends of mine who have wandered have been "found" and have returned home.

We can find the lost sheep and guide them home when we offer them love, acceptance, patience, and assistance — when we emulate the love, acceptance, patience, and assistance that the Savior offers each of us. We will aid one another, and, most important, we will help the Lord in gathering the "lost sheep," when we reach out to those who have been driven away, to those who have had their feelings hurt or their hearts broken, to those who have become spiritually sick. "I will seek that which was lost, and bring again that which was driven away, and will bind up that which was broken, and will strengthen that which was sick" (Ezekiel 34:16).

My friend Janette wandered but was found. I will be forever grateful for her return. But I cannot reach Richard nor many of my other "lost" friends. If you are near them, please love them, never giving up in your efforts to reach them, and guide them home. I will try to do the same for you and your friends. With the Lord's help, we'll find them and be able to rejoice together.

Seek After These Things

We believe in being honest, true, chaste, benevolent, vir-tuous, and in doing good to all men; indeed, we may say that we follow the admonition of Paul—We believe all things, we hope all things, we have endured many things, and hope to be able to endure all things. If there is anything virtuous, lovely, or of good report or praiseworthy, we seek after these things.
                    — Article of Faith 13

This time the challenge was different, and infinitely more difficult: this time, the teenager was my son.

It had been a rough month. My sweet, semiobedient, intelligent eldest son had turned the corner in the teenage years and served notice that trouble was ahead.

Every day brought a new experience: most were not pleasant. John had started to swear. I'd caught him in some lies. He was hanging around with two kids who were not good influences. (I knew these kids from volunteering at school—if there was trouble, they were at the center of it.) Doors got slammed so hard the house shook. I got an argument every time I asked a question or made a request. Every day there was some conflict or altercation.

Of course, ninety-nine percent of these altercations were with me. They occurred almost every afternoon after school and were usually resolved by the time Scott, my husband, came home. I fell into bed at night emotionally spent. I began to dread the time when John came home from school. I realized I was retreating to my room at three o'clock, hoping to get away with a simple question tossed down the stairs, "Hi! How was your day?"

Then the principal called. Could I come to school for a conference? Up to that point, the only conferences I'd had with principals yielded glowing reports about my children's school performances, or they were discussions centered on PTA projects. This time, I could tell, it was not going to be fun.

Sue, the principal, informed me that John had received several warnings from different teachers to stop disrupting classes. He had lost noon hour privileges for throwing big trash cans, complete with trash, down the halls. He had suspended a younger kid by his belt loop from a post and left him stranded there. This time (the final straw) he had been caught throwing books around the library.

I figured a little classroom disruption and hall antics were par for the course in a teenage boy's life, but throwing books? I was appalled. In our house, we loved books, we revered books, we respected books. Each of the children had been taught to care lovingly for books. Each child had his own (and continually growing) library. I couldn't imagine John throwing books!

The principal continued, explaining that John could be suspended from school for this action, because this group of boys had not only thrown books all around the library, but they'd laughed in the librarian's face when she tried to stop them and then they were belligerent with another teacher who tried to intercede.

That night, I confronted John. I told him the principal had

called and that I was going to be at school the next day. I didn't want any surprises: did he have any more bad news for me?

He confessed to a few more unsavory activities, as my stomach churned.

"Why are you choosing to do these things?" I asked. I bit my tongue to keep from saying, "Don't you know better?"

I got the classic teen response: shrugged shoulders and a muttered, "I don't know."

What I knew was that I was going to start shrieking if I continued to sit in the same room with him. I told him I was giving myself some time to think before I reacted. We would talk later.

That night, after much prayer, thought, and planning what to say, I sat down on John's bed and told him I loved him. I told him that we believed in a person's right to make choices. I told him that I didn't understand the choices he'd been making or his motivation. I told him that he was now going to experience the consequences of his decisions.

For a moment, a vulnerable, scared look passed over his face, but then I saw him reset his expression, and he stared at me with cold, gray eyes. Again, I told him I loved him, and then I went to share all this news with my husband, who had just returned home from working late.

The principal had even more news the next day, as my husband and I sat with John in her office. She had spoken with John's teachers, and they all had other concerns. He showed no respect for them or other students. His language was atrocious and offensive. She shared a few quotations with us, and we were shocked. Every teacher had commented on the enormous change they'd witnessed in John over the past few months. Ironically (and thank heavens), his academic work was still okay, though he was doing only enough to get by.

I was frightened. I was thinking about drugs. I was resenting those so-called friends of his who had been such negative influences. I was feeling like a failure as a parent. What was happening with my child?

The principal asked John how he felt.

"Not too good," he mumbled.

"Can you tell us why you're doing these things?"

He nodded.

I awaited his response, and predicted it.

"I just wanted to have fun."

There it was, the answer I'd anticipated. Then John added this surprise, "And I wanted to stop being perfect. Everybody always expects so much from me, and I'm sick of it."

That moment will remain frozen in my memory forever. That was when my heart broke. Here was a child, burdened by his abilities and his potential. He was blessed with a superb intelligence (the school district tracked him in a special program of study). He was an oldest son (of an oldest son, of an oldest son, of an oldest son). He was a bishop's son.

He was my son. "Please, Heavenly Father, guide me, direct me. Help me to help this, thy child." I sent that prayer up through the principal's office ceiling.

The principal gave her verdict: classroom transfers, separating John from his companions in mischief; lunchroom duty for three weeks; no free time for the rest of the semester; weekly appointments with us to track his progress. John seemed to welcome these consequences and agreed to them all.

At home that night, we discussed reasonable expectations and rewards, guidelines, commitments, and consequences. John's suggestions were solid, and, at his request, we drew up a contract with him, and we all signed it.

Then we talked about the notion of perfection. Scott and I

shared experiences when we had made mistakes and learned from them. We assured John of our unconditional love and sent him to bed with warm hugs.

During the following week, John's behavior improved a little. He still argued with me at every turn. That was a challenge for me, but I tried to remain calm and controlled. I tried to discourage his contact with particular friends but to no avail: John would not abandon them.

On Saturday, Scott had to work, and I was committed to speak at a conference. I didn't feel exceptionally qualified to speak about Personal Power, my assigned topic, since my family life was such a mess; however, I'd promised to be there, the programs had been printed, and I had to go.

Before leaving, I gathered the kids for a planning session. I outlined each one's responsibilities to be taken care of while I was gone, and I made a list for them to check. They repeated their job lists to me, so I knew that they understood their assignments. I promised that we'd do something fun when the work was done and I had returned home. Everyone agreed to the plan.

As I drove to the conference, I prayed. "Dear Heavenly Father, we have seen a little progress with John, and I'm grateful for it. But this child is not out of the woods. Please help me to know what I can do. Help me to be a good parent."

Into my mind came a picture of the pencil holder—the one I keep by the phone. I realized that I always reached for a shiny red pencil, one that I bought at Christmastime, though there were many pencils in the holder. This bright red pencil always caught my attention, standing among the plain yellow ones. I liked its sheen and new eraser. I knew that I chose it, every time. I considered bright, colorful new pencils to be one of those small things that brought a bit of sparkle to my daily routines.

Then the Spirit whispered, "Look for the shiny red pencils."

I applied this thought to my relationship with John. If his life was like the group of pencils, then I was certainly not looking for the shiny red ones. Most of the time, I checked for metaphorical broken erasers or points that needed sharpening; I often commented on the stubby pencils that needed to be replaced; rarely, rarely did I look for the bright red pencil in John's "holder."

I was overwhelmed by this realization, and I thanked Heavenly Father for the insight. I promised to apply it in my relationship with John. I'd monitor my statements. I'd look for the positive and accent it. I'd swallow my negative statements, even if I had to choke on them.

Three hours later, I was back in my driveway. It was a dusky, late fall evening. The conference had gone well, and I was relieved to have it behind me. Before I opened the garage, I prayed for help, "Please help me to find something to praise. Let there be a shiny red pencil in John's behavior, and let me recognize it when I see it."

I directed my thoughts to John, as if I could communicate telepathically with him, "Please, honey, give me something to praise."

I went inside the house. The other children had done their work: I could see check marks on their lists. John's list hadn't been touched. I reread the entries on his list: "Gather your laundry/put down chute"; "Walk dog"; "Practice piano"; "Rake and bag leaves in back." I hoped he'd done one thing on this list, at the very least.

Nathan, my second-oldest child, appeared in the kitchen to give his report. I was right: he'd done everything on his list.

I thanked him for his good work and asked, casually, "Where's John?"

"Outside with Craig."

I cringed. John knew the house rule that friends couldn't be there if parents weren't home.

"How long has Craig been here?" I asked Nathan.

"Most of the time you've been gone."

"What have they been doing?"

"Playing basketball. Right now I think they're out on the swing."

I heard laughter outside. The sound of John's and Craig's voices told me they were coming around the house to the front door.

I was so angry and frustrated that I was shaking inside. How could John think he could have Craig here and get away with it? How could he think he could ignore his jobs? How could he be laughing?

I stepped back into the living room to avoid John and Craig and a confrontation. I was so steamed that I needed to cool off or I'd start yelling. I knew that wouldn't help anything.

I took a deep breath, and again I prayed. I wanted to be calm. I wanted to give John the benefit of the doubt, but he was making it so hard. When I opened my eyes, I noticed an old bulletin from church — someone had left it on the buffet. The Articles of Faith were printed on the back of the program. My eyes fell to the thirteenth, and I read it.

That simple verse suddenly meant something new. I realized that this parenting business was all about belief and hope and, especially, endurance. I'd never thought of applying that beautiful verse to parenting tasks.

I reread the last line. For me, at this moment, I knew that this was the very key to success in parenting John: I needed to seek after something virtuous, lovely, of good report, or praise-worthy in his actions.

Calmed, I took another big breath, and walked into the

kitchen. John was standing at the sink, alone, washing his hands. Before I could say a word, he said, "I know I'm not supposed to have anyone in the house when you're not here, but we haven't been in the house, we've been outside, so I thought it would be okay."

He was obviously impressed by his cleverness in getting around the rule. "We walked the dog, and then we played some basketball, and we just finished bagging all the leaves." His voice was full of pride. "I just sent Craig home because it's dinnertime, and I've still got to practice."

I was stunned. He had done almost everything on the list. And I had almost spoiled it all by yelling at him.

"Thanks! I'm so happy to have those leaves bagged. That's a lot of hard work." I was so grateful that I hadn't met him at the door, ranting and raving and accusing him of neglecting his work, for he had brought me a handful of shiny red pencils.

"You must be starved," I said. I was thrilled to the core. We'd had no argument, no fireworks. We were having a normal conversation for the first time in months.

"I'm really hungry," John answered. "What's for dinner?"

"How about going out tonight? I feel a little like celebrating," I replied.

John raised his eyebrows. "You do? What's the occasion? I know, you must have done a good job teaching your seminar."

I chuckled. "It went okay, but what I really want to celebrate tonight is something I learned today. Someday I'll tell you about it."

That crisp, fall evening marked a turning point for us.

John eventually decided that the consequences of getting in trouble destroyed all the "fun" of the moment. Also, he realized that he liked to earn and keep his teachers' respect, so he changed his classroom behavior. He's now a straight-A student.

Determined not to abandon them, he still associates with his old friends, but he's learned to take a stand with them, and I feel that he is a good influence for them. He has also branched out to form many new friendships.

John has made many more wise choices and has enjoyed the positive consequences that come as a result. This process took him a while, but he learned many valuable lessons along the way. I pray he'll keep progressing along this good path.

As a parent, I'm learning to endure all things. As I teach John and my other children, I have discovered it is helpful to heed Paul's advice regarding things "virtuous, lovely, or of good report. . . . " Seeking after these things, I am finding much to praise.

Epilogue

I will impart unto you of my Spirit, which shall enlighten your mind, which shall fill your soul with joy; and then shall ye know, or by this shall you know, all things whatsoever you desire of me, which are pertaining unto things of righteousness, in faith believing in me that you shall receive.

— *Doctrine & Covenants 11:13–14*

It was the last week of December, and as usual, I was up to my eyes in alligators: Christmas thank-you cards, children's vacation activities, the usual run of teenagers dropping by for a visit, food, or advice.

On Tuesday, I treated my Sunday School class to lunch: once again, they'd earned enough points to join me for a special meal at a local restaurant. As I tallied their service points, I heard reports of blood bank volunteering, tutoring middle school students, "being nice to my sister for a whole week," cleaning up after stake dances, massive cookie baking marathons and secret deliveries, good grades at school, and numerous other worthy deeds. Three of my students had so many points that they'd earned the privilege of bringing guests of their own. I was proud of My Kids.

Just before I left for the restaurant, one of the mothers called to complain that her son felt cheated because he couldn't bring a guest.

I couldn't believe it. Here I was going more than the extra mile for these kids, and a parent was complaining! Her son had earned barely enough points to come himself—I'd been very generous with him. I explained my point system to her until I was certain she understood why her son had not earned two meals. When I hung up, that complaint bothered me and diffused my happy anticipation.

The phone rang again. This time it was Jason, asking for a ride. I told him I'd be right over to pick him up.

Jason and I often talked, so he felt free to complain to me about two of the kids in the class. As far as he was concerned, they were total losers. His critical comments also affected me.

Maybe my mind was stuck in negative mode by the time we ate lunch, and maybe we were all too tired, but I noticed all their moans and groans during the meal as well as their inconsiderate treatment of each other and me. Several boys arrived more than an hour late, yet they expected to have their meals served quickly to them. Three kids who had made reservations with me failed to show up—so I had ordered too much food. By the time I said good-bye to them all, I was glad to be rid of them.

I felt better two nights later, however, after I'd had some sleep. On Thursday night, my family held a game night, with an open invitation for anyone to join us. The word spread quickly, and by eight o'clock about thirty kids were in the living room. The evening was a blast—so much fun, in fact, that some of the kids stayed well past midnight. Lucky for me, they finished off all the Christmas leftovers, but did they ever leave a mess! It took me until two in the morning to get order restored.

On Friday, I was so tired I could hardly roll out of bed. I snuggled under the covers for a few extra minutes and reviewed my plans for the day and the challenging New Year's weekend. Because of a stake calling we shared, my husband and I were hosting the stake youth dance on New Year's Eve and a fireside on Sunday night. I realized that I needed to prepare for my Sunday School class *today*. All the classes were changing on Sunday, and I was acquiring seven more teenagers, adding them to my large class of twenty. I decided to prepare my new roll and a fresh set of "Getting to Know You" surveys before the busy weekend hit.

That afternoon, after running a few last-day-of-Christmas-vacation errands, I slumped into my desk chair and pulled out one of my Sunday School lesson manuals. I opened it and looked at my old roll.

A wave of exhaustion swept over me. These kids were wearing me out. How long had I been teaching this Sunday School course? I counted back and realized I was about to begin my fifth year in this calling.

I had to admit that I was maybe getting sick of teenagers. They were egocentric. Needy. One or another was always in a crisis. The cumulative burden of their problems weighed heavily on my shoulders. Could I handle one more kid—much less seven? Could I listen to one more problem or complaint? Could I teach the lessons from my manuals one more time?

No. I was too tired. I had reached burnout. Forget a new Sunday School roll and lesson. Forget the seven new kids. In fact, forget the twenty kids I already taught. I wanted out.

I closed my manual. "Sorry, but I think it's time for a change," I thought, sending the message heavenward. "I'm going to talk to the bishop tomorrow, unless something changes my mind by then."

I'd tell the bishop I was waving a white flag of surrender. If he still felt that I needed to serve in the ward as well as the stake, he could relegate me to a nice, safe corner — working in the library looked good to me right now.

That night, my family piled in the car to drive to the high school to watch the boys' varsity basketball team play. We'd put this game on the calendar during our last family council, and my boys had looked forward to it all week long, so I couldn't disappoint them by pleading exhaustion.

Besides, Jason had made the team, and was eager for me to come and watch him play. I'd get double mileage out of the evening, I told myself: my family would be pleased to go, and Jason would be happy to see me. Mark, one of the kids I was supposed to be welcoming on Sunday — if I were still going to teach, that is — had made the varsity team. I'd heard that he was a talented ball player. It would be fun to see him in action.

Rumor had it that this team was going to be great. I hoped the rumors were true, for our high school had not sent a basketball team to the state tournament in twenty-three years.

The game was terrific: we played the team that had won the state title the year before and was ranked number one in the state again. As the game progressed, the indisputable star of our team was Mark, the one I wasn't going to teach. Watching him play was a pleasure. He was obviously the team leader, a play-maker. He played clean ball. And, unlike some of the other players, he controlled his temper. Even after a bad call against him, one that was crucial to the game, he remained cool. I watched him encourage his team when they gathered for free throws or headed for the huddle. He was a great kid. A real leader. A sparkler.

By the end of the game, which went into overtime, our team had upset the state champs by one point. The crowd went wild.

As we left the game, my fourteen-year-old, Brig, suggested that we go home and make a surprise banner for Mark. These surprise banners had become a family trademark. "If we really hurry, we can make it and hang it on his garage before he gets back from the game!" Brig said.

After we had designed the banner and were waiting for it to print, the phone rang.

"It's for you, Mom." Jeremy handed me the phone. "Don't talk too long."

It was Tom, calling from Idaho. Tom had been in a seminary class I'd taught nine years before. I'd known him since he was in sixth grade and taught him for four years. Tom was calling to share the good news of a friend's engagement.

After we talked about the wedding plans, Tom asked, "So what are you doing these days? Still teaching kids?"

"Yes," I answered. "In fact, as we speak, I'm printing a banner for one of them. My boys are going to put it on his garage in a few minutes. This guy is a fantastic basketball player, and he just won a crucial game. I think he's going to lead our high school team to the state tournament."

I heard myself as I spoke: my possessive words, the joy when I talked about Mark, the pride that registered in my voice.

" 'My Kids,' " Tom said. "I remember when I was one of those. So, Annette, how many kids do you have?"

"Hmm, let me think a minute," I replied. "Hundreds, I guess. I'm supposed to inherit more on Sunday, but, to tell you the truth, I'm debating asking for a release. I don't know if I have what it takes to do this anymore. I'm burned out. Don't you think my bishop ought to release me after I've worked with teenagers all these years?"

"Well, maybe it's time to take a break — hang out in the Relief Society, or something," Tom said.

We talked about his wife, child, and school, until the printer stopped. Mark's banner was ready, and my boys were anxious to go.

I told Tom that I loved him, realizing, as I said the words, how intensely I felt the truth of them, and then we said good-bye.

My family jumped back in the van and we dashed up the hill to post the banner on Mark's garage, trying to be quiet so we wouldn't get caught.

On the way home, Brig announced, "You know what? Mark Pope is my hero."

I thought about that declaration. Brig couldn't have a better role model. Mark was a bright student, a natural leader, a fine musician, a gifted athlete. He was well-liked and respected at school. He was part of a really good family. He was a decent and honest kid. It would be good for my boys to have Mark around our house.

Then my twelve-year-old, Nathan, piped up. "Well, Steve Elder is my hero!"

Steve Elder was one of My Kids currently serving a mission in Korea.

"Why?" my husband asked.

I was anxious to hear the response.

"Because he plays the piano so well, and he's smart, and he's on a mission, and he was a student body officer at Newport, and the girls all like him."

We all laughed. I remembered a statement made by one of Steve's friends when they were both freshmen at BYU. "Steve is a girl-magnet," he'd told us. "He goes into a girls' dorm and sits down at the piano. When he starts playing, the girls come in from every direction. It's amazing!"

I knew this story had helped motivate my boys to keep taking piano lessons, and I thought how grateful I would always be for Steve's wonderful example — as a priesthood holder, a student, a leader, a missionary, a musician, and, yes, a "girl-magnet."

As we pulled back in our driveway, I silently thanked Heavenly Father for providing my sons with good role models. This was more "bread," I realized. My boys were now old enough to benefit directly from associating with the teenagers I taught.

It was nearly eleven before I had everyone in bed. "Tomorrow is going to be a killer," I reminded myself as I walked to my desk to straighten papers and check reminder notes. Shuffling papers, I noticed my Sunday School materials sitting where I'd left them earlier that day.

I picked up the manuals and put them back where I kept them by my scriptures. I thought once again how much I loved those well-worn books. They were not a matched set. I'd bought a new triple combination printed in large type and bound with nice brown leather. I was still working at remarking it because I had found the footnotes to be invaluable. I'd held onto my old seminary Bible, however, even though it wasn't the nicest type published, because it was so well-marked, and brought back wonderful memories whenever I read from its pages.

I stood there holding my beloved Bible and thought of all the things I'd learned from it. I thought of all the lessons I'd been taught, as I was supposedly teaching. I reminded myself why I'd always loved working with teenagers. They were egocentric and emotional; sometimes they did stupid or cruel things, but the best thing about them was they were not *finished* yet—they continued to grow, and they continued to change. Many of my most sublime moments of joy had come from witnessing those miraculous changes.

Then I heard a gentle voice, one I'd come to recognize. It whispered, simply, "Feed my sheep." I did not move. Again, I heard the words. This time they rang through my head. "Feed my sheep."

I knew what I was being told. I could not send up the white flag. Not yet.

I thought about my past experiences as I'd tried to serve the Lord by teaching teenagers. How many times had I been this tired? Countless times. How many times had I cried out for guidance, help, the right words, information about what I should do? Hundreds of times, maybe thousands. How many times had I been assisted, or told what to say to a youth, or given the strength I lacked? Enough times to know the power intrinsic in making covenants and keeping them. "I the Lord, am bound when ye do what I say" (D&C 82:10).

"Okay," I whispered.

I picked up my old class roster and read the names printed there. I looked over the list of my seven new students. I wondered, Which of these kids will be calling me in ten years to share good news? I asked myself, Would I come to love these kids with the same intensity that I'd felt for Tom when he'd called? Probably.

I pulled out a clean roster and typed out a new roll, adding seven more names. When I was finished, I bowed my head and pleaded with Heavenly Father to grant me strength, patience, guidance, and endurance. I rededicated myself to this teaching task, promising to do my best job with these kids, these sheep.

I knew the Lord would help me.

I went to my files and found last year's "Getting to Know You" questionnaires. I needed new questions for this group. I'd ask them to name their favorite music groups, food, books, and cars. I'd ask them about their real-life heroes. I'd ask them what they wanted and needed from this class, and from me. Then I'd ask them to indicate the strength of their testimony of the gospel, using a scale of one-to-ten. I knew I'd be hooked for another year as soon as I read just one paper marked with a "2" in answer to that question. That's all it would take.

I jotted an outline for the first class of the new year and then read the names on the roll again. With a sigh and another plea for heavenly help, I reached deep into my personal reservoir to take another handful of my most precious bread and prepared to toss it out, once again, onto the waters.